DEAD
RECKONING

Howe Sound, taken near Whytecliff Park.
Photo courtesy of Carys Cragg.

DEAD RECKONING

HOW I CAME TO MEET
THE MAN WHO
MURDERED MY FATHER

CARYS CRAGG

ARSENAL PULP PRESS
VANCOUVER

DEAD RECKONING
Copyright © 2017 by Carys Cragg

ARSENAL PULP PRESS
Suite 202 – 211 East Georgia St.
Vancouver, BC V6A 1Z6
Canada
arsenalpulp.com

The publisher gratefully acknowledges the support of the Canada Council for the Arts and the
British Columbia Arts Council for its publishing program, and the Government of Canada,
and the Government of British Columbia (through the Book Publishing Tax Credit Program),
for its publishing activities.

Edited by Robyn So with Linda Field and Brian Lam
Cover and text design (including map) by Oliver McPartlin
Cover Photo: Pixabay

Printed and bound in Canada

Discussion questions for book clubs or classrooms are available at *arsenalpulp.com*.

Library and Archives Canada Cataloguing in Publication:
Cragg, Carys, author
        Dead reckoning : how I came to meet the man who murdered
my father / Carys Cragg.

Issued in print and electronique formats.
ISBN 978-1-55152-697-3 (softcover).—ISBN 978-1-55152-698-0
(HTML)

        1. Cragg, Carys. 2. Cragg, Geoffrey. 3. Klatt, Sheldon.
4. Murder—Alberta—Calgary. 5. Children of murder victims—Canada.
I. Title.

HV6535.C33C34 2017   364.152'309712338   C2017-903897-4
                                                    C2017-903898-2

For my mother—for always, without fail,
getting out of bed in the morning.

BRITISH
COLUMBIA

ALBERTA

● DRUMHELLER
● CALGARY

● VANCOUVER
● SALISH SEA

CONTENTS

DEAD RECKONING:

To attempt to figure out where you are and where you are going based on where you have been.

AUTHOR'S NOTE

Memoir is a particular thing, a story within a story, about a slice of time that has now passed, that has become the past. Memory fades and becomes the present.

To write this memoir—a journey held within a larger, never-ending story—I relied upon a number of people, documents, and experiences to reconstruct the past and as accurate a timeline as possible. I consulted newspapers, day planners, trial proceedings, journals, letters, and notes; I connected with family, friends, and staff; I mined my memories, some vivid, others vague, for relevant moments that tell this story as authentically and truthfully as possible. Memories, inherently flawed, are subjective experiences and are thus authentically truthful.

Time has been woven together but not reorganized so as to misrepresent.

Only relevant passages essential to telling my story are included from the letters between the offender and me; permission was not sought from the offender as this is not his story to give permission for me to tell. Cuts to the letters are made silently. Punctuation has been added where necessary for clarity.

To stay true to the narrative and to respect others' privacy, I do not tell my siblings' stories.

In the end, there is just me. It is my story, my perspective of events. There are other positions and points of view, just not here, in these pages. Those stories are held elsewhere.

More than facts, memoir tells truth. Here is my truth.

S he's a beaut!" a young Geoffrey tells his parents in his audio-recorded letter. He reviews the details of his discovery with precision. "*Tangerine*, a gorgeous red, forty-five length overall, a slim beam."

As she listens to the cassette, she hears, through the hiss of the worn magnetic tape, an excitement in his voice, a playful joy. She can tell he is in love, because it is how he spoke to her mother.

Her mother tells her that after Geoff finished his medical training in New Zealand and began to work as a physician there, he learned to fly planes and got his pilot's licence.

He had never sailed.

But soon after purchasing *Tangerine*, he invites his friends to sail across the Pacific Ocean, back home to Vancouver, Canada. No land in sight. Just a few young men, the stars, a lot of faith, and 1970s technology to get them home.

She returns the tape to the wooden chest filled with his photographs, tools, and other keepsakes. Aimlessly standing in the middle of her bedroom when she should be getting ready to leave with her mother, she remembers his joyful voice, wishing it could fill their house again.

"Just yell," her mother tells her. Her daughter is leaning her shoulder and head against the passenger door, staring out the window into the dense forest of Douglas fir, arbutus, and Western Hemlock as they drive along the road winding away from the marine park where they moved after her father died.

"Just get it out. Yell as hard as you can," her mother says.

"No, I can't. That's not what this is about."

They drive along the on-ramp to the highway, then up to the crest of the highway's curve. She breathes deeply as they reach the summit of Eagleridge Bluffs, looking out to the water where Burrard Inlet meets the Salish Sea.

"Prison is stupid," she says defiantly. She tries to formulate words with her limited vocabulary and adolescent knowledge of the world. "I just wish—" She pauses.

Her mother listens from the driver's seat.

Purpose fills her teenage body as she finds her words. "I wish that everyone who knew Daddy could have something like a device, a buzzer thing." She worries her mother will interpret this as something violent, so she retraces the description. "Nothing hurtful, no. The thousands of people who came to his memorials—all of his family, his friends around the world, all of his patients—we would all get one. And on the other end would be him, the man who killed him.

"Every time we miss Daddy, or want to be near him, or want to tell him something, we could push it," she continues. "For the rest of our lives. And then that guy would know. Then he would know what he took away."

PROLOGUE

Drumheller, Alberta, is a dry and underwhelming place. Its rolling beige hills scattered with farmland, water towers, and bales of hay put me in a reflective mood. Drumheller is known for two things, I'm guessing. One is the Royal Tyrrell Museum of Paleontology, located in the badlands where dinosaurs roamed millions of years ago. When I was a little girl, I visited it, as do 400,000 others each year. More recently, I visited Drumheller's lesser known institution: its prison.

Situated just a few minutes' drive out of town—on Institution Road, no less—medium-security grounds looked as I expected, an image formed in my mind from watching too many episodes of *CSI* and *Law & Order*: massive grey block buildings with a towering chain-fence perimeter. The minimum-security prison grounds, however, surprised me with their lack of fencing and permanent buildings. One-storey residential and administrative portable structures and a large greenhouse were scattered about the open space. In front of the adminstrative buildling, child-size plastic patio chairs sitting in the garden space encircled by a low-rise white-painted chainlink fence caught my attention.

"That's for family visits," my guides, Jennifer and Dave, informed me as we parked in the gravel lot.

We entered the cramped boardroom, and I was surprised to see two windows and lots of light. Jennifer and Dave had prepared me to expect a dull and oppressive atmosphere.

Jennifer, who I guessed was in her late thirties, was dressed plainly and exuded patient warmth. She sat still, calmly, without taking on the gravity of the situation. While I had met her formally only twelve hours earlier, she already knew me well. A restorative justice practitioner, she had read and delivered the letters between me and the man I was about to meet. She always left kind notes on the fax cover pages that accompanied his letters—*Just wanted to check in to see how Carys is doing with all of this,* or *Please let Carys know that he writes about the crime in this letter*—so I knew she cared about me and was there to nurture the process I was about to embark on. Dave, perhaps in his late fifties, is a longtime leader in the field of restorative justice, and he had started walking me through the journey that had brought me here when I met him a year and a half ago, back home in Vancouver, British Columbia, 1,452 kilometers away.

I expected the guards to be unwelcoming. So I was impressed that I could walk right through the entrance, sign in, and go straight to our room. No guards checking pockets or ID. This did not feel like a prison—not that I knew what that felt like. Jennifer and Dave had conducted these kinds of meetings before, and their combined experience eased the worries I had but did not know how to articulate. I had no precedent, no guidebooks, no expectations.

Really, there was no way to prepare myself for the moment the person who changed the course of my life when I was just eleven years old—the person who murdered my father—would walk into the room. All I could think about, waiting there at eight-thirty in the morning, was where the four of us would sit.

Instinctively, I chose the chair facing the door through which this man would enter. I would sit across from him, and the practitioners would sit between us, around the curved end of the boardroom table that took up too much of the room's space. I did not want to appear confrontational by sitting directly across from him, but the small yet significant constraint of the room's size and furniture was all part of that day.

I sat silently in the uncomfortable black office chair affirming my decision to sit here and not in one of the fifteen other chairs surrounding the table, while Jennifer and Dave chatted as they set up the video recording equipment at the opposite end of the room. They came back to their newly assigned seats, and Jennifer informed me about what would transpire over the next twenty minutes of my life.

"Carys, when you're ready, Dave and I will exit the room, go to the guard station, and ask the guards to call him from his room."

I watched her attentively.

"You'll hear his name being spoken over the intercom. Sometimes they say 'offender' or 'inmate.'" This seemed odd to me: they really need reminding of their status in prison? Jennifer noted my reaction and nodded in agreement. "He'll come from his room to the guard station just outside this boardroom within a few minutes. I'll then introduce him to Dave. At that point, either Dave or I can come back to sit with you." She said it like a question.

In that moment, I knew the importance of having a woman sit next to me. Despite having just met Jennifer, I knew she *knew* me. She would help me to feel as comfortable as possible. If I could be myself, I thought, anything that might happen that day would be okay. And if something happened, and I was okay, that would mean I was present in the moment. That day, being present was my only hope for myself.

"You," I replied instinctually.

"So, I'll come back to sit with you. After a few minutes, Dave will knock lightly on the door to see if you're ready to have them both come in. If you're not, that's okay. He'll go back and wait."

"Okay."

"At any point, we can take a break. You tell us what you need. People think they'll be stuck for what to say, but in our experience, the day can fill up quite quickly. We'll be here to guide you, but we know you and think you'll be just fine."

I smiled.

"If you want to end it, just say you're done. You'll know when you're done. You'll just know." She paused and then said, "You just tell us when you're ready."

The room fell silent.

How could I tell if I was ready? I had never considered this question before. How do you make that decision when, for your entire life, things have happened *to you* as opposed to your inviting them in?

I felt my body fill with intensity. Acutely aware of the tingling in my legs, stomach, and arms, I couldn't speak. I had been waiting a long time for this moment and could not believe it was here, waiting for me to be *ready*. I held my breath, and the pressure in my face rose. Tears started streaming down my face.

How could I be *ready* to meet the man who had violently claimed my father's life? The man who had caused me to ask what was the point of life, what was the point of living? This man had brought pain into my joyful world, so much pain that it became familiar. The joy in my life died alongside my father, to be put back together anew but never the same. Death invites people to live.

I looked up at Jennifer, who was sitting patiently. I shrugged my shoulders and lifted my hands up as if to say, "I don't know what's happening."

It occurred to me that I had a choice. I could leave. I'd been intentionally engaging in this process, and it had never occurred to me that I might not go through with it. I wondered if people travelled all this way, across this land, across minds, emotions, and social divides, and then turned back. Had others come this far and then turned around?

"Take your time. You tell us when you're ready." Jennifer seemed to have no expectations, was simply ready for my instruction. I was surprised to be so reassured by her words. She understood and let it be.

I thought of all the people who were waiting by their phones in case I needed them. I thought of those who remained silent about my journey. What would they think? I was so tired of their presence in my mind, having to attend to their needs and questions.

Then I realized that none of these people—neither friends nor family—had done anything like this before. They had no idea what to expect, what would happen, how it would feel. It was just me here. There was no family, no friends. Just me. *I'm here for me,* I thought. And with that, they all left my mind.

Jennifer and Dave sat patiently next to me.

I breathed in and breathed out.

I told myself I could do this.

I would pay attention to what I needed to.

I would say what I needed to.

I would feel what I needed to.

I would be myself.

When embarking on this kind of journey—of restoration, account-ability, and peace—taking a leap of faith seems necessary.

I raised my head to look into Jennifer's eyes, straightened my back as I wiped the tears off my face, and announced: "I'm ready."

Sure, it'll be great," her father says confidently to her mother as they plan their summer vacation with their ten-day-old daughter. "She'll love the motion of the boat."

Soon into their trip, while motoring across the Salish Sea heading for Silva Bay on Gabriola Island, they encounter a storm, a southeasterly wind common to the Salish Sea. Choppy waves come from all directions as rain pelts down. Halfway to their destination in the middle of the open sea, the engine stops, and her father discovers a blockage in the fuel line, a diesel lock.

They know it will take too long to put the sails up by himself and that even if he could it would take too many hours into the night to sail to their destination, where they are to meet their friends.

It is wet and windy above board, so they stay in the cabin. They cannot put their daughter down. With no power, it is too dangerous, as the boat bobs up and down. They must hold her.

"Geoff?" her mother asks, wondering what she can do to help.

"Marion, take Carys to the forepeak and stay there," her father directs her mother. "Don't come out here." Her mother has never witnessed him nervous like this. She sits down with her newborn in the cabin, the driest and most stable space on the boat. As the sun sets, they spend hours in limbo while he repairs the fuel line not once but twice, because it breaks down again.

Many hours late to meet their friends, they eventually dock safely at the marina. One of the worried women cries out, "Why didn't you stay home?"

But her mother has observed Geoff around engines, always building and repairing things. She knows that sailboats are designed not to sink and has faith that he can fix anything.

This will be the first of many summers they will spend in the close quarters of a sailboat, travelling the expansive beauty of British Columbia's coastal waters.

Walking along the docks, both parents gaze down at their newborn daughter cradled in her mother's arms, having just survived their first adventure at sea.

PART ONE

LOCAL
KNOWLEDGE

A sailor's knowledge of local conditions to ensure safe passage.

—Syd Stapleton, Ocean Navigator

A WINDOW 1 OF TIME

The coffee shop was bustling. Customers sat at the rustic farm tables, strangers squished together, ordering coffee and slices of pie. Shannon and I sat across from one another, waiting for our food to arrive.

Despite having known each other at work for six months, acting as youth outreach counsellors for the Child and Youth Mental Health Office in the Ministry of Children and Family Development in Surrey, British Columbia, we hadn't spent time together outside of work. By the time we became good friends, I was balancing two jobs, working half my time with Shannon, and being seconded the rest of the time to the Quality Assurance department, working concurrently as a continuous quality improvement coach and practice analyst. I wanted to work in a quality assurance position full-time, but I knew that would be difficult to achieve. No new jobs had been created since the recession in 2008, around the time I was first hired. I didn't realize how exhausted I was from work, so exhausted that I'd regularly come home, get takeout for dinner, and plop down in front of the television for the rest of the evening. Repeat. Not to mention the hour commute each way. That morning, Shannon had a prenatal appointment at her doctor's office, which was close to my home, and I had the day off from work. We finally managed to find the time to meet as friends.

All new friends eventually ask how my father died. Shannon was no different. I told her that a twenty-two-year-old boy, high on drugs, entered our home intending to rob us and picked up a knife on his way. It was 4:20 in the morning. My father, attempting to protect the lives of his wife and four children, confronted the intruder. In the altercation, he stabbed my father multiple times and left him on the floor, bleeding. The intruder ran away but was caught by the police a day or two later.

I've described the murder so many times it has become rote, as though I'm reciting my list of errands for the day. Sometimes my matter-of-factness worries me, especially when I read the faces of the people as they learn the details of my father's death. *Should I be more upset?* I ask myself, and then realize I am evaluating my behaviour according to someone else's standards. People expect a lot from me: to be sad, to move on, to be well or unwell. I wonder if they know they're pushing their assumptions on me, or if they, in fact, think they are showing compassion. This information—that my father was murdered—is normal to me. It is what happened. I cannot think of my life without it. Of course, I'll tell it like I'm reciting errands.

Shannon responded differently than my other friends.

"Do you know anything about him?" she asked, rubbing her expanding belly without a trace of judgment on her face. Most people cannot hide their horror, disgust, or sensational curiosity. *What is it like to have a father who was murdered?* I imagine them thinking when they look at me with their disoriented expressions. *What is it like* not *to have a father who was murdered?* I want to respond, for this is all I know. Meanwhile, I'm afraid that I'm being judged for something I had no part in but am nonetheless given the responsibility to respond to. I appreciate the nonjudgmental, curious, and gentle existential philosophers of the world. Shannon is one of them.

"He's in prison in Alberta," I said. "He was convicted of second-degree murder and received a life sentence with eligibility to apply for parole after twenty-five years. I was told that twenty-five years was unusual. Ten or fifteen years is the usual period for second-degree murder. I don't know why the judge set parole eligibility at the maximum, but the community and the lawyers in Alberta were angry because he blamed the murder on his friend. My dad had contributed so much to the community—he was a father, an orthopedic surgery resident, a good man." I wondered how this came across, *a good man*. What does that really mean?

"The guy's been moved from maximum to minimum security. There's a photo of him online, from a prison-college partnership with a construction apprenticeship program. He looked big, heavy, like he was protecting himself. My mom told me some things about the trial, like how he lied for a really long time. And after, a former schoolteacher told the police, 'I could see he was bad from early on.' I know things like that." Sharon nodded and smiled.

"He has five years left before he gets an automatic hearing for full parole," I continued. "That doesn't mean he's free, though. I've learned that a life sentence is a life sentence—they'll watch him for the rest of his days."

"I didn't know that," Shannon said.

"Yeah, I've worked in the social services field my entire adult life, and I hardly understand the language the justice system uses," I said, shaking my head. "A few years ago, he applied for an earlier parole date. He applied under the 'faint hope' clause. If prisoners with life sentences have been good, they can apply for permission to shorten their ineligibility times. But his application was denied—he hadn't been telling the truth for long enough, hadn't been off drugs long enough."

I wondered if the people near us could hear our conversation, if they could put together what we were discussing.

"Telling the truth?" Shannon asked.

"Yeah, he lied for a really long time, saying he was breaking into garages with his friend and that his friend killed my dad. The police proved he was alone, though, through alibis, footprints in the dirt around our house, and glove prints on windows. And my mom told me that the police inquired about the possibility that the guy came to our house on purpose, that someone at the hospital may have given him the address. The police never did prove it, but that question has always irked my family." In fact it irked me just to say it aloud, the uncertainty still weighing heavy in my gut.

"Wow. And drugs?"

"I know. How do you get drugs into the prison? Apparently it's not as hard as it seems."

"Did you go to the hearing?"

"No. My mom did and reported back."

I held back my annoyance about how little my mother would tell me. She followed her well-established pattern of sharing only the tip of the iceberg, nothing more, which is troublesome for someone like me who seeks information constantly. From very early on, I've wanted to know why people treat each other the way they do, what causes their behaviour, good and bad. I try to bring attention to glaring problems that are obvious to me, and wonder why no one else seems to care.

I was getting the sense that Shannon wanted the same things I did. I liked it. I liked that someone else was also curious.

"My mom said he's not very smart and that my father's brothers might have been angry about the victim impact statement she wrote for the hearing. She said, 'I hope he's released slowly into the community to learn productive skills, et cetera.' Mom's pretty liberal. At first, I wanted to go to the hearing. Then I realized that the process wasn't for me, it was for him. I was allowed to attend—don't get me wrong, I liked having the choice. But I realized that I wanted more control over the process, not one that's taken over by the legal system, the media, even the psychologists who try to tell you how best to live after trauma."

We laughed. As counsellors for young people, our attitude spoke to a shared resistance to our profession's typical approach to youth as being passive recipients rather than active participants in their lives. We scoffed at the dated theories that were abundant in our field, with academics and professionals keen on compartmentalizing people's emotions, labelling youth as abnormal if their life experiences didn't fit a predetermined, packaged set of orderly stages. My own theory of grief and loss was based on current literature and personal experience: grief isn't only about the death of a loved one; rather, it is the process of building a new life, including a new relationship with the person who was no longer there.

"I've been a 'registered victim' since his first hearing," I said, making air quotes and rolling my eyes at the government's term for my status. "It was weird, though. An old friend of mine said something that really bothered me."

"Oh yeah?" Shannon asked.

I shifted in my seat, unsure how to relay the experience. "I didn't like it at first. He said that as a kid, maybe I'd had the privilege of not knowing what happened to me through an adult lens. I think he meant the trauma of it all."

Shannon grimaced as I continued.

"At first it really bothered me, as though there could be anything good about being eleven years old and having your world crumble to pieces. But I thought about it more, and I figured that he was worried about me seeing the guy at the prison. Like, I would be traumatized because this time I would be processing everything as an adult."

"Do you want to know more?" Shannon asked.

I thought about this question for a moment. Did I? Did I really want to pry the lid off that box?

As a child, I'd had no control over what happened to me. A whirlwind of activity took over my life, and I was forced to witness and experience the dark and traumatic events forced upon me and my family by someone I didn't know. The murder. The search. The trial. The appeals. The murderer, a human being locked away in prison, was attached to my life somehow yet remained a ghost.

Shannon's question made me realize that I could process the information however I wanted. I trusted myself more than anyone else, a skill I had to learn much too young. Now there was an opportunity to approach the situation under my terms—not on terms dictated by Canada's Correctional Service, the parole board, or the criminal justice system.

"Well, maybe there's a way I can meet him that wouldn't be too traumatic," I said.

Shannon smiled and nodded, as though she could envision my future and the kind of peace this decision might bring me.

"I think I have a window of time to do this."

As I said it aloud, I realized that I couldn't *not* go ahead, now that I identified what I wanted.

A thick surgical elastic band loops around her waist, cushioned by her padded one-piece baby blue snowsuit. Her father's hand holds the ends of the band.

Following her father's instructions to make a pie shape with her skis, she points her small boots toward each other, forming a triangle inside his, while they stand in snow at the top of the mountain. The sun beats down on them.

He leans forward, holding his pole horizontally in front of her body.

"Hold this," he instructs.

Reaching out, she places her mittens on the pole and stands tall, reaching just above his waist.

They lean into the slope and begin to descend, swooshing through the powdered snow, their pace quickening as they glide forward, held back only by the resistance of their ski edges dug into the snow. He shifts his weight to turn left, then right, then left again. She follows.

"Okay, Carys," he says encouragingly. He raises his voice to compete with the wind. "Now, let go." Her hands let go. With one hand, he carries his two poles parallel to the ground, and with the other hand he grips the thick elastic band.

She feels the tug of the elastic against her waist, feels the space widen between her and her father. Looking straight down the mountain, she smiles as the wind hits her face.

SOMETHING 2 MISSING

I rushed home from the coffee shop and headed straight to my files. Bankers' boxes stacked and shoved into the corner of my closet contain my university coursework, taxes, journals, and unfinished projects—my paper-hoarding problem. I skimmed past course names, work-program brochures, and playbills, trying to avoid a paper cut. And then I found the two file folders, one labelled Registered Victim, the other Dad.

Opened and unopened letters filled the first folder, letters from the Correctional Service of Canada and from the Parole Board informing me of the offender's escorted leaves from prison. The exact dates, the types of leave—personal development, work, volunteer—and the accompanying form letter, sent repeatedly, from the department's communication officers about my right to access information. There are reports, decisions from the Parole Board as to why his application had not been approved, and many registered victim brochures filled with information on how to attend a parole hearing, what to write in a victim impact statement, and what information about the offender that I had a right to access.

The second folder held photocopies of newspaper clippings from the time of my father's death in 1992, the trial in 1993, and the appeal in 1995. Headlines from the *Calgary Sun* and *Calgary Herald* stare out at me:

Intruder stabs doctor to death

Hunt for killer

Shoeprint left at scene

Suspect charged in doctor's killing

Accused killer fingers best friend for crime

Murder suspect's claim called hoax

Accused killer sticks to story

Murder jury still out

Doctor's murderer sentenced to life term

MD's widow thanks city for support

Murderer appeals sentence

Killer's sentence upheld

How often I had sat in my bedroom when I was a teenager reviewing these clippings. My mother had given some to me when I asked what the newspapers wrote about us. I would hover over the words the journalists used to describe my father and us. "Slain." I hated that word, upset to think of my father that way. "Doing well." Was that a good thing? *What if I wasn't well?* I wondered. *Would that be okay, too?*

Much later, it occurred to me to ask my mother if she had more information in her files, and she gave me copies of the medical and coroner's reports. I saw where the nurses and surgeons marked the stab wounds on his body, and I read the detailed descriptions of their minute-by-minute interventions. I learned that at the hospital emergency, Dad was able to tell the doctor that the pain was horrible. Maybe these were his last words, and I wondered how afraid he may have been, how much pain he was in before he lost consciousness. I hoped he had been comforted that his friends took care of him during the last moments he was alive. Sometimes I sat hovering over the clippings for hours, sometimes only for a few minutes, but I always went back to them, continually trying to process what had happened to me, what had happened to my father.

Nineteen years later, sitting cross-legged in my closet, I looked at the opened and unopened stack of form letters from communications officers that I'd collected over the years, since I'd learned that I could also receive the information sent to my mother by requesting to become a registered victim with the Parole Board of Canada.

"We can just send the information through your mother," one communications officer said when she noticed I had the same address as my mother.

"No," I told her firmly. "I'd like them addressed to me." I was offended that she assumed she could send such significant information through my mother. I also wondered why I hadn't been told of this right to become a registered victim when I turned nineteen, wondered why the system left it up to my mother to share this information with me. *The system doesn't account for families' diverse communication styles*, I thought. *Or did the officer just want to save on paperwork?*

"My mother doesn't tell me all details," I wanted to say to her, but I assumed she wouldn't understand my complaint. *The system doesn't seem to understand that children grow up and want to know things that their parents may not have been forthcoming about.*

I used to receive phone calls from communications officers as early as 8:30 in the morning. Finding it disruptive to receive their news before going to work, I opted for letters summarizing the information instead. Soon I tired of that too, form letters arriving, often weekly, in unmarked envelopes: thin ones I kept in a pile, unopened; thick ones I opened. When I told this to my family, they asked why I wanted to keep getting them. "Because I have a right to the information," I replied, if and when I wanted to read it. But information such as escorted absences on such-and-such a day for whatever reason, when he was permitted to leave the prison grounds, wasn't necessarily what I wanted. I wanted to know things outside the scope of these letters, things not covered in the relevant legislative acts.

I picked up the files, grabbed my computer, a pad of paper, and a pen, and headed to the patio where I spread files, photos, and clippings out on the table. I lived in a basement suite on Vancouver's North Shore in my mother's best friend's house, overlooking English Bay and Stanley Park. Making myself comfortable, warmed by the late afternoon sun and eased by the placid view of the water, I began to envision a plan.

No manual exists on how to contact the person who ruined your life. It seemed apt, because despite the uncertainty and the risk, I'd never been one to take guidance. Rather, I liked to do things on my own.

But I couldn't do this alone—randomly contact my father's murderer; that would surely not be recommended or even allowed. I began to search "restorative justice" online. Having worked in social services for some time, I knew that programs connecting victims and offenders existed. A number of websites, video links, and articles came up on the screen. I scanned the articles but was soon bored with the jargon that was meant for a justice practitioner audience.

I settled on a poorly filmed documentary about the journey that two women, a daughter and her grandmother, took to meet the man who murdered the daughter's mother. I watched the daughter stare into the offender's eyes while he repeated her mother's last words as he held the gun to her forehead: God will forgive you. *The daughter would never have known that if she hadn't taken the step to meet him*, I thought. Interesting, too, that the men in their lives had not wanted them to meet the offender. Their discomfort had been palpable, I noted. I tucked that information away for another time.

I went back to the files. All the contact information scattered on the table in front of me left me at a loss about where to start. I decided to email the one person who might know exactly what my next step could be.

Katy, I began, after finding her contact information online.

> I don't know if you recall, but we met after a presentation you did at the University of Victoria in the spring of 2005. We had a brief conversation. I am the daughter of an amazing man who was murdered by a young man in Calgary, in 1992, during a break-and-enter into my family's home. He is now in prison. I was eleven years old at the time. Your ideas of restorative justice and compassion are central to my life and how I have responded to this injustice. I am now a youth counsellor working with young people and their families.

I recalled her presentation, the story of her husband's murder. On New Year's Eve, he had walked to a neighbour's home, whose kids' party was out of control. In his attempt to intervene, he was beaten to death, and for five years the town stayed silent about who was responsible. As I listened, tears streamed down my face. The connections to my story were profound: murder, a young man, drugs, the omission of truth.

> The reason for hoping to reconnect with you is that I want to understand, learn, process, and integrate the events and circumstances connected to my father's death. I feel that this is the next step, to integrate this experience into my life.

I asked if she was available to talk.

After pressing Send, I left a message for the Victim Services office. "I'm a registered victim, Carys Cragg, and I'd like to learn more about restorative justice. I'm not sure if I'm calling the right number, but I'm wondering if you could put me in touch with the restorative justice people, someone in Alberta, where the crime took place, or in BC, where I live now …"

Before I could compose the next email, the phone rang. A 250 area code was on the display, from Victoria. It was Katy.

"Thank you so much for getting in touch," I said. I was floored by the generosity of this woman, whom I'd spoken to for two minutes in a hallway, for taking the time to call.

"I do remember meeting you," she said. "Oh, how lovely to hear that you're considering this journey."

I held my chest in gratitude, both for the calming attentiveness in her voice and her recognition of what I was about to do.

"You must go directly to Community Justice Initiatives. Dave and Sandi are the restorative justice facilitators there." I jotted down their names. "They're the most wonderful people to take you through the journey."

"How are your children?" I asked, curious to know about their trajectories after their father was murdered when they were only toddlers.

"Oh, they're just wonderful." She then told me about her teenaged daughter being a spoken word poet and that I should look for her videos online. She wished me well on my journey and to contact her anytime.

I immediately found her daughter's videos. In one, she performed a piece about her father's murderer. In another, she discussed her artwork and letters she got from audience members, written to the murderer at her request. *At only sixteen years old,* I thought. I admired her strength.

After receiving a message from a Victim Services officer directing me to contact the coordinator of the Correctional Service of Canada Restorative Opportunities program, I emailed one last inquiry, this one to the organization Katy recommended, the Community Justice Initiatives Association.

I had put it out into the world now. All I could do was wait for their responses.

I poured myself a glass of wine and pushed aside the files, photos, and clippings and opened my laptop again. Now that I'd identified my desire to do this, I needed to ask myself why I wanted to do it.

Why would I want to contact my father's murderer? After all these years, why not just leave it be? I was safe and well, with a circle of friends and family around me. I had worked hard to get where I was, and was doing good work. At the top of a blank document, I wrote: *Why am I doing this?*

> To learn more about what happened to me twenty years ago.
> To acknowledge the presence of a ghost.
> To face the unknown; I want to stop imagining.

Contacting this man, at this time, was no neutral act. As such, I was afraid I'd have to face opposition and resistance from those close to me. I'd be conjuring up old memories, old pain. It was risky. Surely I would need good reasons to justify what I was doing to myself and others.

> To engage in a process I can control.
> To learn about him. Who is he? What was his life like before?
> What is it like now?
> To learn what I am like with this new information.
> To tell him who I am.

Something big was missing. I'd grieved the loss of my father, and it had left a scar on my soul. I was proud of surviving, even as I was sad at having survived. And I was sad for my younger self's flawed and lonely, painful efforts to go on living. But I hadn't addressed my feelings about the murderer.

Here was this man, living in prison, who had disrupted my world to its core, and all I knew about him were the simple facts I'd been told as a child. The doors of possibility were open, and more reasons flowed through me in a torrent.

Because I am well.

Because it will be right.

Because only the other side of the story gets told—the trial, the offender's defence—and that's not my story.

Now I was getting somewhere. I took a sip from my glass of wine and glanced up at the eagles soaring overhead.

"The eagles," Mom used to say, "are Geoff looking over us."

We've always lived close to where eagles make the tops of the trees their lookouts. Whenever my mother felt sad and was missing my father, she would spot an eagle overhead and know he was there.

But I wanted more than an eagle. Long ago, I decided to right the wrong that took my father away from me when I needed him most, so I wrote to him. I would sit by the water's edge and write, listening to the crash of waves against the rocky cliffs, near the place we had moved back to after his death.

These were the waters that held our family's history. The ocean saved my life, giving me what it had given my father: constancy. He learned to navigate it and to master its depths. When I was younger, I'd go outside to the backyard perched about forty feet above the ocean, and stare out to the sea and surrounding islands. I'd tell myself that I was okay, that life would be okay. No one and nothing could assure me of this as successfully as the ocean. Its salty smell, the sound of waves crashing into the cliffs, the wind against my skin—the water took care of me when no one else could. We were all forced to survive.

And now on a different patio near the water, more relaxed and calm than I had been in years, I returned to my list.

> To be closer to my dad, to know this part of his life.
> To take care of my younger self.

I pulled out the clipping with my father's photograph prominently displayed. It was the picture used in most of the news reports during the city-wide search, arrest, trial, and appeal. My father stands in his white physician's coat, smiling gently at a patient.

"Well, Dad," I said aloud, raising my glass up to the sky. "I'm going to do this. What do you think?"

I smiled to myself. I knew I'd be okay.

Shortly after her seventh birthday, at the end of the school year, they prepare to move to Calgary, Alberta. Her father has accepted a position in the orthopedics residency program at the university. Her parents pack up the moving truck and station wagon and they drive the twelve-hour route from Vancouver across British Columbia and through the Rocky Mountains, with a few stops along the way. They stop to stretch their legs and get a bite to eat in Kamloops. When they cross the border into Alberta, they break for family photos at Lake Louise. In the photos, she and her mother and siblings sit cross-legged, leaning into one another. Kneeling behind them, her father stretches his arms to place his hands on their shoulders, forming a triangle that matches the inverted triangle of the mountains reflecting in the shimmering waters of the lake behind them. They look happy.

They make it to Calgary by nightfall.

As they enter their new home, a split-level house, the kids start exploring. Some head to the basement, some to the yard and back in again. They pick their rooms and get excited, hoping they will soon meet the kids next door. For their first night in the house, the parents position the mattresses in the living room, cover them with sheets and blankets, and together the family sleeps: child, parent, child, child, parent, child.

DIFFICULT 3 WORK

I placed my hand on the door handle and the metal blinds clanked against the glass as the door opened toward me. An unassuming, one-storey, poorly marked building on a side street not too far from the town centre, it was like many of the nonprofit organizations in the community that I visited on a daily basis as part of my job as a youth outreach counsellor, where I'd meet my clients.

"I'm Carys. I have an appointment with Dave."

As the receptionist stood up, I could feel the tightness in my chest. I had spent the past thirty minutes driving east from my office in Surrey to the Community Justice Initiatives' office in Langley. Along the way, I couldn't stop my train of thought. *What will this meeting be like? What will I have to watch out for? What do they know and not know that will influence our interaction?*

After being escorted through the building, I sat on the side of the table's curve with a view of the door. It was a small makeshift boardroom typical of underfunded nonprofits: temporary interior walls constructed twenty years ago, a circular table taking up half the space, uncomfortable chairs, stale air, an old television in the corner, and mismatched particle-board shelving units filled with program brochures and psychology literature. Light entered the space through slim horizontal windows near the ceiling.

Dave entered the room. "It's great to meet you, Carys," he said, shaking my hand. "I'll find Sandi and get your file." Moments later, they returned to the room, sat down, and placed a thin file on the table.

Dave's casual dress and friendly demeanour were reassuring to me as we began our conversation. His nasal voice reminded me of a radio host on CBC, comforting and distracting at the same time. Sandi was slight in appearance, with thin blonde-grey short hair and a soft voice. She seemed to prefer to sit back and observe, rather than lead as Dave did. A good team, I thought.

"We're so glad Katy told you to find us," Dave began, to break the ice. "Like I said in our email exchange, she's one of our adopted family members."

"All roads lead to the CJI," I joked. "Eventually, the folks in the Prairies told me to contact this office too. So here we are."

Dave spoke about his long-time experience in the restorative justice field, conveying a certain kind of confidence he'd had to defend over the years, like a cowboy in a new frontier. "It can be confusing when the offender and victims live in different provinces. Rest assured, we work with people across the globe," he said.

Knowing the scope of their work experience made me feel more confident. And I was comforted that the multiple inquiries I'd sent that weekend had all directed me to the same office.

As Dave reviewed the assocation's programs, he used common terms that I'd seen on his organization's website. "You're familiar with the criminal justice system, as you've been through the trial, and so on. It's governed by retributive justice, where crime is a violation of the state, defined by lawbreaking and guilt. Justice determines blame and administers pain in a contest between the offender and the state directed by systematic rules."

I lingered over the words "between the offender and the state."

"Here, we operate by a different worldview: restorative justice. Where crime is a violation of people and relationships, the violation creates obligations to make things right. Justice involves the victim, the offender, and the community in a search for solutions that promote repair, reconciliation, and reassurance."

Here, I thought, *my needs will be represented.*

"So, you're thinking of being in contact with the person responsible for your father's death," he said.

An interesting turn of phrase. Not "murderer," "offender," "felon," or "convict."

"Yes. I don't know what that could look like," I said, despite having done a preliminary review of my options online. I always come prepared, likely fueled by some kind of perfectionist-anxiety tendencies. I wanted to know what they might say so I could thoroughly process it and be able to respond effectively. They had knowledge I wanted, knowledge of a system I was largely unfamiliar with.

"Every case is different," Dave said. "Over the twenty-plus years of this program's existence, we've met with offenders convicted of a range of crimes. Petty theft, breaking and entering, assault, murder. We have trained a number of workers across the country. Sandi and I deal with the most violent cases in the region through our offices."

I knew he was including me in that reference, and I was pleased that he recognized the significance of my case. I wanted to trust that he and Sandi could anticipate the questions I might have and the problems that might arise. After all, this wasn't petty theft where the offender agreed to do community service to repair the trust destroyed between teenager and local retail clerk. This was murder.

I realized about halfway through the meeting that I was putting Dave and Sandi through a test. Although I didn't have the option of working with other facilitators, I nonetheless observed their words and demeanour, assessing what it would be like to spend time with them at my most vulnerable.

"What options do victims have?" I asked.

"Well, some people want to meet the person right off the bat," he said. "We prepare both parties for that meeting. Some people just want us to support them through the parole hearings. Some want to send a message, wanting no response in return. Some want to write for a period of time and never meet in person. There are many options. It's up to you to decide."

"I was thinking that I'd like to meet him, but not right now. Maybe write to him first, tell him who I am." I paused and then asked, "How often do prisoners agree to things like this?"

"Both have to agree. You'd be surprised. In my experience, the majority, even the most violent offenders, agree."

"Really?"

"At first they feel like they owe their victims everything," he said. "So they seem to agree out of obligation. But they all seem to benefit, even if they feel bad for benefiting from something like this, because they know they've hurt their victims so much. I should also say at this point that the victim-offender mediation process doesn't impact the parole hearings. It's not allowed to influence that process."

"Oh. Well, that's good to know. That would be a massive conflict of interest," I said.

"Through the process, they learn that not all victims want them to suffer, which can be quite different from their experience thus far," he continued.

"I've always known since my father died that the man who killed him didn't have what I had—family, opportunities, wellness. When I turned the age he was when he killed my dad, I was going to university, surrounded by new friends, and attending classes. When he killed my dad, he was messed up with drugs and gangs and was breaking into homes. You don't do that when you've had a life of being cared for."

"You work in the field, yes?"

"I'm an outreach counsellor, mostly for kids in the care of the Ministry."

"Ah, we've got a pro on our hands." Dave glanced at Sandi, and she smiled.

"Well, I don't know about that," I said. "I've always known what I needed or was missing or wrong. But it never occurred to me before now to do this."

"You've come to the right place."

"So what happens next?"

"We have our counterparts near Drumheller. They'll visit him and ask if he'd be okay with receiving a letter from one of his victims. We won't tell him which one."

"There are many," I said. "How would my letter get to him?"

"You'd send it to us, and we'd forward it to our people in Edmonton, which is the office closest to Drumheller Institution, and they'd take the letter to the prison and hand it to him. Any response would come back through the same people."

"Who are these people again?"

"Well, there's Sandi and me here. And Jennifer in Edmonton, in the program there."

"So all of you would read my words before he sees the letter." I wondered how intrusive that would feel.

"Yes. We wouldn't check or change anything. We're there to let you know if there's anything concerning. We'll introduce you to Jennifer soon. Meanwhile, you can think about what you want to do."

I sat with the information, silent. Forty-five minutes had passed. I was surprised that there was so much to take in, so much to consider. I had the distinct impression that Dave and Sandi were caring people. They didn't position themselves as counsellors yet had showed me great interpersonal skills. While I thought that they understood the gravity of what was happening here, I sensed that they weren't necessarily on my side, but nor were they on *his* side. They gave the appearance of being neutral: They weren't there to open doors, speak for me, or tell me what to think. They were there to walk alongside me.

Then a question occurred to me. "Don't you have to give me some sort of psychological testing to see if I'm okay to go through this process?" I asked.

They smiled, perhaps in response to my sarcastic tone. "We just did."

She hops out of the car and runs into the convenience store just a few minutes' drive from their house. They've stopped to pick up candy and magazines. Her dad trails in.

"Find me some purple licorice," he requests from the counter as she stands in the aisle, reaching up as far as she can to put an assortment of candies in a small plastic bag. She scans the shelves for it, which has become her favourite candy, reminding her of their trips in the dinghy to the remote island stores during summers on her family's sailboat.

She returns to the counter with a bag filled to the brim, and while the attendant counts out the pieces, her dad asks her, "What magazine would you like?"

She looks past the teenage fan magazines and the comic books, trying to find the one she knows she likes. Lifting it off the shelf, she asks, "Can I get this?"

He takes the magazine out of her hands and flips through the pages. "It's full of cabins, full of floor plans of cabins," he says quizzically.

"I like them," she replies, and pictures the one in her bedroom, the pages filled in as though it were a colouring book, with beds, couches, and tables. She sketches the future homes that she imagines she will live in, and when she is done, she returns to the particle-board dollhouses her father built for her and her sisters. She puts the dolls aside and spends hours rearranging the furniture.

"Okay," he says as he places it atop their items for purchase, where a pack of cigarettes has mysteriously appeared.

"Don't tell your mom," he says playfully.

"You're not supposed to smoke, Daddy," she reminds him as they leave the store.

PART TWO

UNDERWAY

Said of a ship that has just started after getting her anchor.

—W. Clark Russell, *Sailors' Language: A Collection of Sea-terms and Their Defintions*

A GHOST

A couple of weeks passed and I hadn't heard anything from Dave or Sandi. I sat in my office, wheeled my chair to the door to close it, and stared at the large painting hanging above my desk.

It was something I had copied from an oil painting I'd seen in a design shop, something I could never have afforded. Instead, I'd bought some cheap sample wall paint and a large canvas and began to re-create it: horizontal stripes blending into one another, streaks of white and black paint that blended into grey. Colleagues tried to guess what it represented as they passed my door. "Vancouver's clouds?" the administrative staff suggested. "Your clients' minds?" the counsellers asked. But in truth, the painting came to represent the grey system in which I worked, trying to serve the best interests of my clients. Grey indeed.

I heard doors open and close around me, people shuffling in the hallways going about their very busy days. Clients to see, meetings to facilitate, reports to file. I worked in a bustling facility where those involved in child protection, youth guardianship, family development, and mental health services were connected together in a maze of offices linked by the building's central lunchroom, a room I avoided at all costs. That's where the social workers, clinicians, and other social service workers ate and gossiped about the weather, healthy eating, and broken diets, among other mundane topics.

But they also gossiped and complained about clients. It was not uncommon for a family to seek help from multiple services—protection, counselling—at the same time. I hated the lack of professionalism of workers who discussed clients without any regard for the clients themselves.

"God, she's exhausting," someone would say.

"She's so bipolar."

"Manipulative kid, can you believe he did that again?"

"Deadbeat."

Is that how counsellors, police, or journalists gossiped about my family in their lunchrooms? I thought to myself. I wanted to ask them, "Is that really how you think about the people you serve? What if clients were to walk by and overhear?" So I avoided the lunchroom, likely appearing antisocial by doing so.

I refocused on my task at hand and wondered why Dave or Jennifer hadn't been in contact. I was under the impression that Jennifer had met with the offender the previous week. Turning to my computer, I composed an email to Dave and Sandi: *I'm wondering if you've heard?*

By the end of the week, they still hadn't replied, and among my weekly home visits, school consultations, and clients' psychiatric sessions, I became concerned. What if he had said no?

I didn't want to begin a letter if he was going to say no. But I couldn't help myself. I'd begun to scratch sentences of what I might say to him. A small pile of scrap paper collected.

The absurdity of it—that I hoped for my father's murderer to agree to accept my letter—was not lost on me. That I might need something from him put me in a position of dependence. It was an uneasy feeling—a paradox I did *not* like.

Sandi finally replied by email, saying that both she and Dave had been out of town at conferences, and then wrote at length about family matters, which made me wonder why she was disclosing so much about her personal life. In my work, I'd been taught to only disclose personal matters that helped clients move forward. But, then again, she wasn't a counsellor. I read on.

He is willing to participate in the process.

We could begin.

She said that while she hadn't taken notes from their phone conversation with Jennifer in Edmonton, this is what she remembered.

He was a bit nervous about the idea of communicating with you through this process but he is open to it. It sounded like part of his anxiety is based on victim impact statements that others have written. It is common for offenders to question whether someone they have harmed can feel anything other than anger and bitterness. A letter exchange might be a good and necessary next step.

I was at a loss for words, as I'd never considered him this way. *He is willing. He is nervous.* It's not that I'd imagined him devoid of feelings. Rather, he was a ghost who had wreaked havoc upon my world. He existed in my mind as a mysterious, empty, untouchable, intangible thing. Not a monster. Not a murderer. Not a killer. A ghost. How could he be anything else? I was eleven years old at the time. I never saw him; we hardly spoke of him. I never imagined what I would say to him. That part of my father's death had been sealed up tight—by my family, by the legal process, and by the culture around me.

That I could cause him to experience anxiety had never occurred to me before. That within this anxiety—worrying who might want to inflict pain on him, or get restitution, or whatever it was that he was apprehensive about—he had decided to agree made him even more human to me.

"He is a person," I said aloud to myself, staring at the grey painting on the wall. I noted to myself that this was the first thing I'd received back from this process: the fact that he had become a person.

In my reply to Sandi, I agreed to begin with a letter.

> I'm sure he would appreciate knowing about me and my intentions, as I am aware of the horrible things some of my extended family have written and said to him. I stand on the opposite side of the spectrum.

I promptly followed up with an email to Dave asking for more details of their conversation with Jennifer—how the request was presented to the offender, what the offender said, how Jennifer interpreted the conversation, and what the facilitators thought. I was in the process of writing a letter, I told him, and ended the email with a question of timelines—*How quickly is it delivered? How will you let me know if/when he responds to a letter I send?*

Dave replied a few days later, saying that he'd try to make time to speak with me that afternoon but that he might not be able to because he was in court with the mother of a murdered son, at the trial of the accused. I thought this was sharing too much—had he let his other clients know that he was meeting with the daughter of a murdered doctor when he was busy with me?

As I began to write the letter, I wondered how to introduce myself while also conveying that I was not like my extended family or, more specifically, my father's brothers? My uncles' story—not just theirs but angry people's in general—always gets told. Their voices are always heard. But why? Because they're louder, more forceful? Since my father died, I had attempted to develop an articulate voice, and I often found myself dominated by angry voices, sometimes even my own, when it had gotten the better of me.

What words would I use to convey to him that I was unsure of the process I'd like to engage in, but that I wanted to be in contact nonetheless?

I realized that I shouldn't get ahead of myself, not try to plan out every little detail.

I began with his name.

May 1, 2011

Dear Sheldon,

My understanding is that Jennifer visited you in early April to ask you if you would be willing to participate in communicating with me. I've been informed that you are willing to participate but curious to know who is making this request and that you may be somewhat apprehensive due to past victim statements made by some of my extended family members. When I learned of this information, you became a person to me instead of an abstract concept as you have existed in my mind for 19 years, and as a result of this inquiry, I am even more compelled to be in contact with you, whatever that ends up looking like. I appreciate your openness.

I have many things I'd like to say, ask, clarify, and under-stand—but for this letter, I'd like to introduce myself and clarify my intentions of requesting that Jennifer meet with you. I know that they are called restorative justice practitioners. I don't really care what anyone calls this process—dialogue or whatever. I'm more interested in just acknowledging that our life paths have crossed in an extremely significant way and, at least for me, to go on in life without acknowledging that connection would be living a less than full life. I will assume you know very little about me—or even that I exist—and I know very little about you, which is one of the reasons why I would like to be in communication with you.

My name is Carys and I am the eldest daughter of Geoffrey Cragg, the person whose death you are responsible for. I was 11 years old when you came into my house and shattered my world into pieces. Naturally, I have an 11-year-old's understanding of what happened that morning and of the events that happened afterward. Now, I have to admit, I was a sophisticated 11-year-old, so I was extremely inquisitive and that continues today; however, people only tell you certain things, and there is a limited degree of access to information at that age, no matter how many questions I may have asked. My family, community, and society have avoided the subject matter of what you've done, and everything related to that. We've wanted to move forward. I feel that some information about my life is stuck at that age and I'm trying to interpret it as an adult, which doesn't really work without learning the information as an adult. I'd like to change that.

In order for you to feel more comfortable about this process, I'm hoping that you can ask me what you'd like to know about me, in order to proceed forward. I feel compelled to say at the outset that I have no feelings of hate, rage, or anger toward you, but rather, I have a profound need to understand who you are, and what you were doing, so that I can integrate that information into my life now.

I was invited to the most recent hearing; however I was not

in a place where I wanted to write a victim impact statement
for the hearing, nor did I attend because I felt it was a situation
controlled by someone else and I want to have a say about how
my life looks and what I am exposed to. I was informed afterward
that some of the content of the statements were hateful in nature.
That is not who I am, nor do I associate with those particular
people. I do hope that you knowing this clarifies that particular
aspect of me contacting you.

I'm wondering if it would be okay if we send a few letters back
and forth for a bit of time. I don't know about your preferences,
but I like to write letters as I feel it provides a safe space for
expressing oneself and it provides calmness and patience when
it comes time to reading them.

If it is okay to request, I hope you can respond to a few initial
questions of mine and please feel free to ask me some questions
of your own:

- What was it like for you to be asked by Jennifer to engage
  in this process?
- How come you've agreed to engage in this process?
- Is there anything you'd like to request from me that would
  make you feel more comfortable about engaging in this
  process?
- Is there anything you'd like to share with me that you believe
  would make me feel more comfortable about engaging in
  this process?
- Have you ever wondered how I'm doing after all these years?

Thank you in advance for responding to my questions. I look forward
to your response.

Regards,

Carys

I reread the letter before sending it off to the facilitators I was entrusting to take it to him. Looking at the scraps of paper on which I had scratched ideas and sentences since meeting Dave and Sandi, I made sure I'd covered everything I wanted to in the first letter. I'd keep the rest for another time. I was aware that I was being polite, kind, and concerned with his willingness to participate, but I figured the opposite would surely shut down the possibility of a response.

Now that I'd begun, I was even more determined to get what I wanted.

She walks down the stairs, feeling the shag carpet between her bare toes as she heads toward the office in the corner of the basement. She knows she shouldn't bother him. He's studying for school, but she wants to see him anyway. She passes the furnace room and smells the freshly shaved wood, catching a glimpse of the half-constructed violin on the table, her father's latest hobby.

"Daddy," she says quietly as she gently pushes the door open.

He lifts his head from the open book on his desk. "Hi, sweetie," he says. He rolls his chair toward the door, leans forward to pick her up, and sits her on his lap.

She looks at the piles of books stacked high on his desk, the pads of paper with his familiar messy doctor's handwriting, and the various protractors, compasses, and rulers lying about. She picks up the two-point compass and holds its metal legs. "What is this for?" Avoiding the point at the end of one leg, she touches the pencil lead on the other.

"That's for when we go sailing," he says. He places the point on a pad of paper and swings the other leg around in a circle. "To find our way to where we want to go."

She raises her head to look at the the large corkboard above his desk. Her gaze lingers over the photos pinned there. They've been sequenced together to create a panoramic collage. From left to right, in the foreground she sees moss-covered rocky ground, arbutus trees, and craggy cliffs dropping down to the ocean. There is midnight-blue water and white-tipped waves that lead her eyes to a number of islands along the horizon. Behind them, mountains shift from green to blue as they fade into the distance, meeting the pastel-hued sky.

She looks at her father.

"That's called Howe Sound. I'm going to build a house for us there," he says with a wide grin. "That's where we'll live when I finish school, and we go back home."

NOWHERE THAT
WAS MINE

I sat in the CJI boardroom once again. Dave placed my file on the table, pulled the letter out, and slid it across to me. Sandi sat next to him. I shuffled in my seat and held the letter's edges as it lay on the table. Their eyes were on me and my eyes were on the letter. It occurred to me that they'd watched thousands of victims sit here across from them, reading correspondence from the person who ruined their lives.

"So, you've read this, yes?"

They nodded.

"It's—" I paused. "—okay?"

What other word could I have chosen to convey my ambivalence? *Safe? Conflictual? Hurtful? Untrue? Authentic?* "Okay" would suffice because, really, how would Dave and Sandi know? They facilitated the process, told me what they'd learned from thousands of these interactions, but they knew nothing about the offender and what he'd been thinking for the past nineteen years.

They nodded.

"I just read it here? You'll be here with me?" I asked. I surveyed the dull room and was glad that I'd agreed to read it there and nowhere else. Not my house, not my office, the car, the coffee shop—nowhere that was mine. I didn't want whatever energy might come from the letters to be in my safe places until I knew I was safe in these letters too.

"Yes. I may step out for a second, but we're here," Dave assured me.

"Then here goes."

I lifted the pages, noting the numbers in the top left-hand corner of the fax cover sheet. Sent May 19, 2011, 5:07 p.m., from an Alberta number. I thought of the people this letter had travelled through: from the offender in a prison meeting room, it had been handed to Jennifer, faxed from Edmonton to Dave in Langley, then handed to me across a table.

When I first learned that a series of people would be reading the offender's letters before I did, I thought it would be invasive, that it might change what I wrote. But as soon as I held the letter, I was satisfied knowing that they had read both my words and his, and that if they needed to flag something for me, they would, and that they could and would catch me if I fell.

Leaning into the letter, my forearms resting on the table's edge, I caught myself holding my breath tightly. The paper weighed heavy in my hands.

The typed font was dense, seemed less than single-spaced. *May 16 20011*, it was dated; I determined to overlook its typos. The letter began just like every letter I've received.

Dear Carys,

He began by telling me how Jennifer had approached him, how he was *surprised and apprehensive*. His first concern was that he *didn't want to deal with any kind of confrontational retribution or witch hunt*. He said Jennifer had assured him this was not the case. He wrote that he accepted my invitation to open lines of communication. *This is the least* he could do.

Let me comment on how well spoken and bright you seem to be, he wrote, and this made me slightly uncomfortable, made me shift in my seat.

On that note, he stated, he knew my *intentions are not malicious in any way*, but for his own sake *I must ask you a number of questions*. This was because he'd had *some not so good experiences*.

As soon as I read the phrase, I knew exactly who he was talking about. At the offender's first—and, thus far, only—hearing, for escorted temporary leaves from the prison, my father's brothers had been quite angry toward him, blaming him for everything that had gone wrong in their lives, despite the fact that they'd been angry and miserable long before my father died.

I was reminded of a story my mother had told me about them.

"How did they all get from Vancouver to Calgary so quickly?" I asked her one day.

"My parents and sisters, and your dad's parents and brothers, after learning of the break-in and stabbing, were at the Vancouver airport waiting for the plane to Calgary," she said. "When they learned that he died, they began to fight, yelling and arguing with each other."

"Really? But Dad just died."

"Your grandfather, who never raised his voice, began to yell at them. 'You three get your act together,' he told them. 'My daughter and her four children don't have a father anymore. There are other people to care for now.'"

But they never did offer us any care—not to my mother who had the unfathomable task of getting up every morning and caring for four fatherless children, not to my siblings and me entrusted with the task of trying to live again. Then again, if they'd offered, my mother likely wouldn't have taken them up on it, because they would have tried to exert power over us for something as little as a meal or a ride to school.

Are you a very religious person and do you think I need
salvation? Are you affiliated with any kind of media? Do you
need information for a novel or thesis that you will be sharing
with another party? Are you currently in therapy and need
some kind of closure? Are you a psychologist or psychiatrist?
Are you affiliated with any law enforcement?

As I scanned his list of cautious, potentially accusatory, questions,
I wondered why he was asking them. They bothered me because they
seemed to be seeking protection or safety, some assurance of my intent.
But what about my own safety? I was contacting the person who had
killed the most important person in the world to me—surely, his safety
was irrelevant.

What if I answered yes to any of his questions? Would that preclude
me from being in contact with him? I wondered if these types of people
had approached prisoners in the past and passed judgment over them,
and word had gotten around. But judgment, I reflected, was at the
core of the entire matter. I thought of my intent as I'd described it in
my letter to him:

I feel that some information about my life is stuck at that age
and I'm trying to interpret it as an adult, which doesn't really
work without learning the information as an adult … I have
a profound need to understand who you are, who you were,
and what you are doing so that I can integrate that information
into my life now.

I realized I would have to explain myself more clearly.

If this situation were reversed, however, and he were contacting
me out of the blue, I reflected on the questions I might ask him in

response, which might sound judgmental and self-protective in nature too, like: What does rehabilitation mean to you? Are you apologetic for your crimes? Have you stopped trafficking drugs in the prison? Have you stopped lying about who murdered my father? How did you pick our house? Have you proven yourself to be a good, productive person, despite your horrific extended list of destructive incidents of drug abuse, assaults, break-and-enter charges, incarcerations, and general antisocial behaviour? Have you changed?

But these weren't the questions I wanted answered, not yet. Nor would I have believed his initial responses. No, I was learning, having read his questions, that, in fact, I wanted to ask different questions. And I was learning that was okay: I could do whatever I wanted, write what I wished. No one could tell me what I should be doing, not even him.

So, I wondered, why should my father's murderer have the right to a sense of security in these letters when that security was so violently taken away from me? Ironic, I thought, given the circumstances, and continued to read.

> I would like to let you know how truly repentant I am for the
> things that I have done in my life, but this is not the proper
> format for me to express this to you. I want you to know that
> I have taken a long hard look at myself over the past few years,
> and came to the realization that honesty with myself and others
> have brought me where I am today.

Honesty. Really? A few years? How about nineteen years? What had he been doing the other sixteen years?

With that I hope that you are prepared for what I tell you.

And I hoped that he was prepared for what I would tell him.

> Also I want you to know that I am a product of my environment, and that some of the things that I say over the course of our conversations, may be brutally honest. I do agree with you that our lives did come crashing together, not by choice mind you, but by the selfish greed and drug-dependent common criminal that broke into your house that night, and murdered your father. The details of this will come out in time. I first have to be certain of your intentions. As you probably already know, I have had dealings with your uncles in the past, and they have expressed cruel intentions. This is not inconceivable to understand, considering what I have done.
>
> I would like to share that I think about you your mom and your siblings all the time. I heard through a family member that your mother had remarried and moved out to BC. I don't know much more about what kind of upbringing you had, and I have no idea how your step father was. I often thought that considering how special your mother was, stepping out with her liberal beliefs, that you guys would be guided in the right direction. But I see that you have reached an impasse in your life which needs to be addressed.

I hated that he incorrectly stated my mother had remarried and moved out to BC, as if it happened in that order and in one fell swoop. We moved to BC a few weeks after the trial, and she remarried thirteen years later. *Those are my people, not yours,* I thought indignantly. *I get to think about them, you don't.*

What did he mean, that he thought about us all the time? I suspected that he likely only learned about my family through newspaper articles or court proceedings. Perhaps the family member he referred to had searched for and seen my mother's new last name. Perhaps they had forwarded him newspaper clippings from a few years back, when we'd taken the money left over from the generous collection for our undergraduate tuitions and donated it to our elementary school's library and music room. My siblings and I were described in the article, and I wondered if he had access to that.

I wondered what he meant by *guided in the right direction*. How condescending, as though he hoped someone had swooped in and taken care of our traumatized selves, put out the fire he'd started. His own mother had most likely not guided him in the right direction, I thought. Then I wondered if his mother would feel protective and disgusted with me if she learned I was thinking about her.

So let me speak on what I am doing today and have been doing for the past few years. Right now I am currently restoring 2 churches in a community in Alberta. Before that I was working at the local recycling plant here in Drumheller. Right before that I was working for a nonprofit organization building homes for single mothers in need of affordable shelter. There is a sense of accomplishment when you see the final product and listen to others comment on how this is going to help them. I enjoy listening to music, walking and playing my guitar. I'm working towards my eventual release right now and striving to gain as much knowledge as possible to help me be successful and make better choices. This letter is starting to sound like a parole application for some reason. I do sometimes think about how hard life will be out there. I am scared, but also thinking that with the proper guidance I hope to be successful. But I know that it will be a significant struggle. I am a very quiet reserved person and sometimes wary of others intentions. Since my life is so public I tend to be a bit Apprehensive. Once I am comfortable in knowing that this is on the up and up, I will have no problem sharing my life with you.

I clenched my teeth at the resumé he'd just given me. *Make better choices.* To become a better man, or to get out of prison? Ironic, I thought, that he was building and maintaining homes when he'd ruined mine. I wondered if he ever thought of that.

I would like to pass the torch to you now, whatever you feel comfortable in telling me about what you do, what you have done, what you intend to get out of this would be greatly appreciated. The courage it must have taken for you to write me is staggering. You probably have a lot of disconcerting ideas about what took place that night and I do hope that I can shed some light on them. What is it that compelled you to write to me? What would you like to get out of corresponding with me? I can only hope that I can give you what you need. If there is anything in particular that you want me to share please don't hesitate to ask me.

Thank you for reaching out.

Sheldon.

His name, I'd seen it so many times before, however, never addressed to me.

I raised my head and looked at Dave and Sandi across the table. The fluorescent overhead lighting seemed to brighten, and it hurt my eyes. I was quiet for a moment, which they respected with their silence, then I said, "Huh. So there it is. There you go."

"What do you think?" they asked.

"Why was he asking all those questions about priests, psychologists, journalists, and police?"

"He's likely heard of someone being judged in this way. Or someone hasn't treated him well."

"It did sound like a parole application, like he was trying to prove something. I'm glad he said that it sounded that way." I paused to think. "I didn't like the spelling mistakes," I said, and laughed at myself for paying attention to such things. "But ..." I wasn't sure how to say it. "God. My uncles, my dad's brothers. Why does what they do get to be what happens? I can't stand being around them. Sorry."

"He mentions them. Something happened?"

"I wouldn't be surprised if they've been really aggressive toward him. But I don't care about them. I care that their actions could influence what I'm doing here." I imagined they'd be angry if they knew about this. I singled out my father's brothers, but really it was my father's entire family.

All of a sudden, memories started flooding my mind.

"Mom, I remember Daddy crying one night. How come? He never cried."

"That was when your dad's parents wrote a really awful letter to him, blaming him for lots of things that were going wrong in their family. Money issues, mostly."

"Nana and Grandpa?" I asked, confused.

"I was leaving the driveway one day, and his parents slammed their fists on my car door window, saying I'd ruined their family, that it was my fault he was leaving Vancouver."

"They did that to you, Mom?"

"He was in the family medical practice for fifteen years, with his father. They had a lot of land investments together. He left it all to go back to school."

I scrunched my face, sad for my father.

"When your dad was accepted to Calgary's orthopedic residency program, and he was deciding what do to, I told him, 'I didn't marry a land developer. I married a physician.' So we moved. His family didn't like that he moved away."

My aunt asked my mother to attend my grandfather's funeral service in his home; my mother asked me to go with her so that she wouldn't be alone. I reluctantly listened to my father's brothers' speeches in which they idiolized my father and their father, and I wondered if the other people at the service knew how the family treated each other when no one was watching. One of my uncles described his disbelief that his sister didn't show up to their father's service, as though she were obligated. They hadn't seen her in over twenty years, after some conflict that remains a mystery. Everyone seemed to leave each other in that family. I stood at the back of the room, surveying them with disdain. I wondered which of these traits I might have seen in my father if I'd known him as I grew older. I wondered why he seemed so different from them.

I was sure they'd see the act of contacting my father's murderer as something that got in their way. But I no longer wanted to think about them and tried to put them out of my mind. "Do people tell their families?" I asked.

"It's different for everyone. Some tell immediately. Some tell along the way. Some never tell. They keep it to themselves forever."

"Oh, I'm sure that I'll tell my family soon," I said. "I just want to see how this goes first. So, what happens next?" I asked.

"What do you want to do?" Dave asked.

I told them I would write another letter, but that I would email it to them. They said they would alert me to his response, and we would meet again at that time.

Walking back to my car, I felt a trace of self-assurance I didn't recognize. I walked a little taller, felt a little lighter, like I had done something I was meant to do but didn't know I was meant to until I started.

Before I got in my car to begin the commute home, I looked up at the sky and smiled. "What have I started?"

I laughed at the strange nature of the situation, knowing in my heart I was one step closer to my dad.

She feels an itch in her throat. She is next to her father, watching. A woman with long blonde hair and dressed in loose clothing stands next to a stool, holding a microphone in her hand. Darkness surrounds them as they sit in their front-row theatre chairs in the small auditorium in the hospital where her father works. The woman begins to sing. Her strong voice resonates inside the walls of the room.

Her parents take her to shows on special occasions. *The Nutcracker* one Christmas, *A Christmas Carol* the year before. They take her to see friends' daughters in their high school productions. In her ballet and singing classes, she imagines herself as them. She is artistic and expressive, and her father likes that. He likes to hear her sing.

Trying to get rid of the itch in her throat, she coughs, then coughs again. Her dad places his warm hand on her back, rubbing gently.

She doesn't listen to the words, just the sounds of the lady's voice, and she wishes she could sing like her one day. She wishes she could stand up in front of a crowd of people and calm them with the sound of her voice, make them feel more alive. In her lessons, when she has to perform and compete, she is nervous with the lights glaring down on her face, standing in front of all the staring people. She always forgets her words.

She is unable to stop coughing and begins to feel embarrassed.

Between songs, the performer lifts her glass of water off the stool and brings it to her.

"Hi, sweetheart. Have a sip of this," the woman says kindly.

She takes a sip and feels the rush of cold water stream down her itchy throat. It relaxes her. She feels her father's warmth beside her.

As they exit the building after the show and head to her father's car, he asks, "Did you like it?" She grins.

"Are you going to sing like that one day?" he asks encouragingly.

She raises her eyebrows, her eyes wide open. He hugs her tight, then opens the car door.

NOT  KNOWING

Each of his reflections had set off new tangents of thought in me. Spring turned into summer, and I accumulated ideas for my next letter. One evening I came home from a family gathering, sat on the couch with my computer on a pillow on my lap, and wrote.

June 19, 2011
Sheldon,

Thank you for writing back so promptly. I can appreciate your inquiry as to my intentions. I'll do my best here to clarify.

I am not a religious person and do not believe in salvation or any version thereof. I'm not affiliated with media. I'm not seeking information from you for a novel or thesis. I'm not in therapy and I do not believe in any concept of closure. I'm not a psychologist or psychiatrist, but I work quite closely with those professions. I am not affiliated with any law enforcement.

I am a child and youth care practitioner, currently working as an outreach counsellor and case manager with children, youth, and their families who struggle with mental health and related problems in a social and economically impoverished suburb near Vancouver. I love my work and the people I work with.

The third to last question requires more of a response. It's a great question. Why not go on living my life without the acknowledgment or knowledge of you? One of my responses is: why not? People whose loved ones have died of cancer get to walk for a cure, donate to and participate in charities, etc. What do I get to do? Violence and its effects on so-called victims is basically silenced past the point of a trial and I think this is unjust—in addition to the unjust act of murder itself. I want to participate in what happened to me, not be a passive recipient.

To be honest, I don't know what is going to come of this conversation we're engaged in. Acknowledging your presence is a good first step. I believe I would like to meet you one day, if you're okay with that, as the written word calls for certain topics and in-person calls for other topics.

So why would I want to build rapport with the man who murdered my father? Because you altered my life so dramatically, so completely and entirely, that I need to know you, what happened according to you that night, what led to what happened, how you make sense of what happened, how you feel about it now, etc. I want to incorporate that into my existing understandings of that night and the aftermath. I do not like how our society separates people in our situation. The missing piece of the puzzle is you.

I write to you just a few days after my 30th birthday. I'm very excited to be 30 as life seems to be getting better and better, which I'm quite proud to say, as the first 10 years after my dad died were quite horrible despite things looking quite successful on the surface. I've had the privilege and opportunity to do my Bachelor and Master of Arts degrees in Human and Social Development and Child and Youth Care. I like writing, reading, people watching, cooking, arts and culture events, and interior design.

I also write to you on Father's Day. My dad and I used to celebrate my birthday and Father's Day on the same day. We have an unbreakable connection—he is like me and I am like him. The day is really no different than any other day—a continued reminder of wondering how my dad would be participating in my life, what kinds of conversations we'd have, what we'd share together, how he'd support me, and so on. I've actively attempted to create a relationship with my dad after his death and this is what's made me able to be myself. As you have learned, I now have what I like to call a deputy dad.

Writing to you on this day makes me wonder whether you are able to celebrate with your father, in whatever form that takes, whether you have a father, whether you are in contact with him. I wonder if you have family in your life and friends who adore you, who take care of you and you take care of them, whatever that looks like. I wonder what connection you have with the outside-of-prison world, in addition to the work you described earlier. I wonder what life is like in prison, what occupies your time. I'm curious to know what guidance you are seeking to make life outside of prison successful, as you mentioned, and what scared means to you. I will not assume anything.

Thank you for acknowledging the courage it's taken for me to contact you. I thank you for taking the same risk, of not knowing.

Regards,

Carys

Only a few weeks had passed when I received an email from Dave indicating that Sheldon had written a letter. He asked how I'd like to receive it. I opted for fax and asked that he send it to me at work.

I paced the office hallway waiting for it.

I promise to not read it at home or work, I wrote in my response to Dave when he confirmed that he'd sent the fax. I walked to the fax machine again and watched the familiar cover letter appear.

Facsimile Transmittal. Community Justice Initiatives. 4 pages. Private & Confidential. For the named recipient only. I appreciated Dave's attention to privacy.

I walked swiftly back to my office, slid the letter into my bag, and got back to work, feeling calmer now that I had the letter. As I finished up the day's reports—mental health specialist responses to critical incident and injury reports of kids in the care of the Ministry—I thought of where I should read the letter. I didn't want to read it at work—too distracting. And I certainly didn't want to read it at home—too unsafe. Home was for sleeping, cooking, reading, writing, lounging. It was not for reading letters from my father's murderer.

On the way home, a few minutes before my highway offramp, I turned into a mall parking lot and contemplated my options. Forcing myself to choose, I walked into a restaurant, asked for the corner booth, and ordered a glass of wine. It was five-thirty and wasn't too busy yet. I looked around, noticing the men in business suits sitting at the bar watching a game, the busy servers dressed in their skin-tight black dresses, and the diners in the booths along the window in front of me. From the corner of the lounge, I could see everything.

Shhhhh, don't tell your mom," he says as he stands on the garage workbench and lifts the box up to the exposed ceiling rafters. He balances the box across two beams.

"What is it?" she asks.

The scent of old machinery, wood shavings, and car exhaust surrounds them in the cold garage. She shivers as she watches him climb down.

"It's for Christmas. It's a serger for your mom," he says proudly.

"A serger?"

"A sewing machine. See?" He steps closer and shows her the inside of his T-shirt hem.

She stares, confused, raising her eyebrows and scrunching her nose.

"And it goes really fast," he says enthusiastically, just as he would describe any of the tools sitting behind him on the table that spans the width of the garage wall: wood planers, table saws, drills, and block clamps. With them he has made violins, flying foxes, dollhouses, hot tubs, and a cabin on Sakinaw Lake.

He likes to make things.

UPBRINGING

R emoving the letter from my bag, I placed it on the table and took a sip of wine. With my thumb and forefinger, I touched the left side and bottom edge of the letter to line it up with the woodgrain on the tabletop. I lifted the fax cover page and began to read.

June 29, 2011

To Carys.

Hello once again and thank you for clearing things up for me. I was trying to not only find out a little more about your intentions but to try and ease my own insecurities as to why you have revealed yourself to me. With that I think that we can continue to communicate with each other for as long as you feel comfy.

Where I am at today with my life has some dissimilarity from where I was at in life when I was a young man. Mind you, I still have my moments of immaturity. I am 41 years old but tend to get along with younger men rather than older men. I relate to their plight more. I find that the younger lads will listen to my story and maybe get something out of it. I have been on the inside for a long time now and have gained a lot of respect. I want to tell you that I admire you for what you do there are a lot of kids that do need the guidance you provide. I was kind of a wayward kid myself and could have benefited from such direction.

As I scanned his words, I wondered what version of himself he was showing me, just as I had shown him a version of myself. I'd reread the letter I wrote to him and laughed at the professional veil I had constructed around me—partly strategic, partly in self-interest, and partly for self-protection.

Let me tell you a little about my upbringing. From what I can remember about my childhood there was not enough food in the cupboards, but always seemed that there was always enough money for drinking. Along with the drinking came violence from my father towards my mom. I really don't want to call him my father because all he is to me is a shadowy figure that yelled screamed and punched my mother in the face. When the time came I was actually glad that he was gone, but he did in hindsight create a new monster in his wake. Which was my lonely dejected mother that didn't know what to do with theses feelings she had coursing through her heart. So she did what she thought was best, and started on this journey to find another hopeful candidate to father her children and take care of her needs as well?

Some of these candidates tried to tame the monster and others fed the fire from which she grew. From that fire came a death of a little brother and countless beat downs for the other two that were left. I would like to tell you that my mother thought she was doing what was best when she had us shipped to other relatives for the summer holidays so that she could get her carousing ways out of her system. But we were just toddlers at the time and thought that this was the way things were done plus we didn't mind as long as we were not there. It was fun in the sun happy go lucky and all that jazz, then we had to go home. What we came home to was a mother so happy to see us that it put a smile on my face you couldn't wipe off with a steel grinder. After about a week or so the drinking started again and there was strange men appearing. So I thought to myself, if they won't leave then I will. So I started to run away from home. Now this is not what led me to where I am today, this is just a catalyst of me running away from home and having my first run in with the law. I know that there are a lot of kids out there that are much worse off than I was but that was my life and my experiences and in my mind at the time it couldn't have been any worse.

"Exactly," I said aloud, directed at no one in particular and at everyone at the same time. As I heard myself say the word, I extended my hand, as if gesturing to make a point to some invisible person sitting across from me. I shook my head, reminded of the youth currently on my caseload.

I thought of one older youth, living on her own, getting into fights because she had nothing better to do, most of her family having given up on her a long time ago and those still around using her to bring them drugs and alcohol; the preteen boy living with his father who couldn't sustain a job or a home past a month or two; the teenage mom whose young children were in other people's care, who couldn't focus her attention on one subject for more than five minutes, let alone build the capacity to gain custody of her children again. I thought of their dire conditions and the relative futility of my service to facilitate change.

I shook my head in disappointment; his story confirmed so many assumptions I had made—that he was born into horrible conditions to people whose best care would never be enough, where his solution to run away opened more doors that began a life of trouble with the law.

With my palm cradling my forehead and my elbow on the table, I stared at his words. I had the distinct impression that murdering my father was but one of a series of horrible circumstances-turned-choices he had made as a result of what he'd endured.

So on a brighter note I do have some things that make me content here at the institution. I own two guitars and I am self-taught, I like to play video games and cook and watch TV on certain days. I did work hard towards education I've managed to take some college courses here at the institution. I went and took a trade in carpentry. I work in the community for the most part and really enjoy meeting new people. It's funny that you said you like to watch people. This is what I find myself doing every time that I am out in the community. I would be sitting down for lunch and see these people driving walking biking and I catch myself staring trying to figure out how they live strive and coexist with their environment.

When I do meet new people they seem to be a bit stand offish because they know where I came from. This is a small community here in Drumheller and when someone "convict" goes to work out in town our employers know exactly where we come from. Sometimes I meet nice people that are in acceptance that people come from all walks of life and realize that what they did in their pasts don't necessarily define who they are today. In my case, I know that the crime I committed will always define who I am. I try to conduct my behaviour in a manner that they will soon come to a conclusion that I am not this scary monster. Today there are many lifers out on parole, striving to live their lives with the little dignity they have left. My eventual release scares the living hell out of me.

I looked up at my surroundings, having been immersed in the letter for some time, and listened to the familiar clinking of cutlery, the chatter, the welcoming of new patrons. Perhaps this wasn't the best place to read a letter, and I felt slightly embarrassed that I'd brought such a thing into this place. I held my forefinger where I'd left off. His words lingered. *Coexist. Lifers. Dignity. Release.* They sat heavy on my chest, loaded with meaning, nothing I could process there in that moment.

I have some acquaintances here but nobody that I would call a friend. I find it very lonely now but will manage. I have to stay here because as you are probably aware I'm trying to get my sentence reduced so that I may be eligible for a parole a couple of years earlier than my scheduled dates. This is not a new trial, this is only a hearing to decide weather or not I have earned the right to be released due to the fact that I have demonstrated behaviour to warrant such a release. Always under scrutiny! I only want to try to make my life better, selfish as it may seem. I have to try to heal the wounds that I have caused without opening new or old ones.

This is why I decided to involve myself in this process. I am not an angry person I hold no animosity towards your family and I did not go to your home to murder anybody. So why would I not agree to this. I owe you everything that you have asked for and more.

I wish that I can let you know how confused I truly was. I'm not talking about drugs, those just fuelled the fire that was me at the time ... I still need to work on some of my thought development.

For example, just the other day I was mediating a situation between a few individuals. Things got a little out of hand and I was attacked in the gym. I should never had gotten involved but what does someone do when you see some poor kid who knows not what he says sometimes is about to meet his maker. Three individuals decided to take offence to what was said and to confront him. I saw this taking place and put myself between theses individuals and this kid, Bad choice! I was later told that I should have just left this kid to his vices. This is how fast things spiral out of control when you choose not to do your own time. I live in a minimum security house this shit is not supposed to happen here. I do not want any kind of sympathy from you I just want to give you an idea about what it is like here.

I hope this letter has been informative for you, it should give you a kind of idea about who I am. It's amazing that the things I fear the most are out there and if I am correct the person you fear the most is here. I would like to change that; I can stare down three men willing to tear into me with reckless abandonment. But I cannot look you in the eye if I ever saw you face to face. I hope that we can change that before we ever meet. This process that we are in right now is so compelling to me I have to see it through. So thank you for taking this courageous step, and including me.

Sincerilly [sic], Sheldon.

I paused, a little confused by some of his wording and disappointed with some of his conclusions, yet surprised by his ability to reflect. Then sadness took over. I could have told myself that I was feeling sad for him, for the world created for him, for the world he then created for himself. But I found myself sad that this man's life, the darkness of which I could only imagine, was so incredibly unfair, and because no one was capable of caring for him, my dad had crossed his destructive path and died.

When do we become responsible for our own lives? Can we survive the social conditions we are forced to endure, then make something better? And is better ever good enough? Since my dad died, I'd asked myself these questions, sitting in high school classrooms, studying at university, and working in the social services field. Sheldon's story told me that everything I'd assumed, questioned, and worried about—everything I knew—was true.

Her father leans against the kitchen counter, picks up a fork, and digs into the steaming hot, bubbling browned edges of the homemade macaroni and cheese, always with extra cheese, and places it in his mouth. She and her siblings sit at the table a few feet away.

"Marion, this is delicious," her father proclaims. Before he finishes his mouthful, he places his arm around her mother's waist and kisses her.

"Yuk!" she and her siblings yell in unison and quickly turn their heads away.

"That's it, on Friday we're going to cook for you," her father announces.

"Oh, Geoff, what fun!" her mother says. Delight spreads across her face. He is always at work or school, and she is always taking care of them. They all look forward to Friday night.

PUT BACK
TOGETHER AGAIN

I didn't notice it coming, the change that began to take root. It started with food.

I had developed a bad habit of picking up takeout food on the way home from work, and never in my thirty years had I learned to properly cook. Now, I decided I would spend my Saturdays researching recipes, shopping for ingredients at the Granville Island Public Market, trying to follow the recipe instructions, and then finally, sitting down to enjoy the meal. I prepared everything at the start: chopping, measuring, grouping ingredients together. Focused on the preparation and soothed by the constant attention, stirring, and monitoring, my mind didn't wander anywhere. Cooking took up the entire day, and for the first time I didn't care. It made me present.

Weekday evenings, I began to attend events around town, such as author readings in the basement of the Vancouver Public Library and shows by performance artists on obscure stages. I sat in booths at Cafe Deux Soleils on Commercial Drive, compelled by the slam poetry, and wandered the various rooms of the Vancouver Art Gallery. Afterwards, I would write about what the events inspired in me, how I hadn't felt this creative since I was younger.

I would also wander the aisles of Chapters' massive magazine section, picking out my favourite design magazines from around the world. I brought them home and flipped through them as I sat on the floor, tearing out pages that looked interesting which I collected in a binder, a reminder when I was a little girl imagining my future home filled with all of my favourite furniture, placed just how I wanted it.

One day in early summer, while seated on my living room floor, I looked around at all the furniture in my apartment, furniture that was not mine. I went through my binder of tear-sheets of favourite couches, consoles, coffee tables, rugs, and lighting, and got annoyed with myself for never getting any of the beautiful things I'd dreamed of.

On a whim I jumped in my car and drove to a mid-century modern furniture shop, the one I'd occasionally visit to touch the fabrics and see the new trends. One couch in particular caught my eye, which I ended up buying. That same weekend, I got a low-standing, circular marble coffee table, a larger console to hold my pottery collection, design magazines, and television, and a tall, slim, watermelon-coloured side table. The living room of my dreams was becoming a reality.

Soon I found myself hosting more dinners for friends. I spent more time lounging. I walked with more confidence through my home.

These hobbies were liberating, yet I felt guilty for not being more productive at work, as my family had raised me to strive for. Succeeding at school and then in our developing careers were the measures of success, if only due to the absence of all other topics in our family conversations. No one spoke about their plans for a random week-end morning. Instead, we spoke about getting second degrees and promotions.

"Just do your best," my mother would say. I was a perfectionist, and she tried to support my goals, never questioning my constant need to improve. But with no internal compass for deciding what was enough, and in the absence of anything else unrelated to work or school, somehow I internalized the message: *You could be doing better, you could be doing more.* This dictum had a stranglehold on me, and I couldn't release myself from it.

That summer, a colleague and friend recommended I apply for a teaching contract at her college—nothing big, just supervising a handful of students while they did practicums at various social services agencies around town. I despised interviews, but this one was different. Though I was the youngest person in the room, I felt as though the panelists were my peers. We talked about our practices in child and youth care and shared similar beliefs about what kids needed in order to grow up well.

"All youth work should be outreach. Why we make kids show up to offices is beyond me," I said to the panel.

My ideas about counselling and my views on the mental health system, child welfare, holistic child- and youth-care practice, and out-reach work were all welcome. They didn't recoil at the avid articulation of my progressive views. Rather, they delighted in it, and I knew I'd come to the right place.

"It's a small practicum contract," one interviewer said. "You'll meet with a handful of students around town to discuss practice issues and their professional development, providing feedback where needed. And give an evening class once a week."

A short while later, I received a call to confirm I'd be starting soon. I liked where things were heading. I knew I was taking on too much, but the work at the college intrigued me.

Late that summer, Dave nudged me with an email. Jennifer would be visiting Sheldon and if I had a letter ready, she could take it: *No pressure.* His gentle deadline motivated me. When it came down to it, I never really wanted to write a letter. Sure, I wanted to send the letter, but "want" wasn't quite the right word. I didn't want a murdered father. I didn't want to grieve his loss. I didn't want to put my life back together again. But these were the circumstances I found myself in, so yes, I wanted to write a letter.

August 28, 2011

Sheldon,

Thank you for your thoughtful and reflective letter. While I wanted to respond earlier, life has been quite busy; however, I see the light at the end of the tunnel, thank goodness.

The busyness occupying my life is multiple jobs, all of which are creative and challenging but exhausting nonetheless. I appreciate that you say you admire what I do, but more often than not I wonder what my work is all about. What am I attempting to do when I meet with young people who are attempting to survive in harsh and oppressive conditions? Should I not be contributing my time and energy towards changing the very conditions in which they live—poverty, exploitation, generational violence and trauma? I study a lot about this—the policies of our government, the practices of our professionals who say they have the best interests of young people, when I really don't think they do. I think they just want to brush the problems under the table so it 'looks' like our society is functioning well. I am told by many people around me, 'We need people like you' and 'Oh, I couldn't do the work you do' and 'How do you do it?' I find these statements offensive—condescending—they could be helping people rise up out of their harsh conditions, rather they contribute to the very conditions that exist.

The world you describe of your upbringing is quite similar

to the young people I work with every day. I feel so powerless to assist them so that they might have more opportunity to engage in activities that feel creative, resourceful, and contribute to their health and well-being. What would you tell me to do with these young people who have experienced horrors, atrocities, and oppressive acts committed against them? What would you tell me to say to them that would offer glimpses of a life that they would enjoy, thrive, and be successful?

What you did, how our lives came crashing together, propelled me to wonder about the injustices of the world. At first, I was focused on the injustice of murder—and its effect on my functioning. The events that occurred as a result were almost equally unjust—financial changes, moving cities and schools, losing friends, conflicts within my family, my mother forced into a position of surviving and keeping us housed, fed, and clothed, starting anew again when just 11 years old. I believe I did a damn good job of making the best of it, but I resent having to do it in the first place. I wonder who I might have been if this had not happened to me. Perhaps you've had those thoughts of yourself and your life as well?

I feel connected to the way you describe watching people. I wonder what people are thinking, how they figure out their days, why they've chosen to do what they're doing. I also feel connected to the way you said, when you meet people in Drumheller, that people know you're a 'convict.' Ironically enough, during my youth, I felt a similar way. People knew that my dad was murdered. They interpreted me with this always in the back of their minds. When I moved away for university, to a new city, to new people, I could redefine who I was. I could tell them on my own terms, once I trusted they had my best interests in mind. This, I felt, was liberating.

You mention that you're always under scrutiny. Do you have any freedom from that, to just exist as a human being without the gaze of people's judgment? I am peripherally aware of your parole dates. Your dates remind me of how long it's been without my dad physically present in my life. I get letters from the Victim Services staff saying when you have escorted day visits out in the community. I have a stack of these letters. I knew about the last hearing. Perhaps I'll be ready to go to the next one.

In the later part of your letter you describe a conflict where you stood up for a younger person in prison, and you were told by the staff to just leave it alone. I'm shocked by their interpretation of the events you describe. To me, you've stood on the side of the less powerful person and actively attempted to protect him. In my opinion, if I were to leave a less powerful person to the hurtful intentions of others, that choice would be unjust. I wonder how the person you stood up for feels about your actions? Appreciative? Like he has someone on his side?

I promise you, what I fear the most in life is not you, but rather it is losing people I love in circumstances of which I have no control. If we ever meet face to face, I hope that fear is not an emotion that is in the room.

When you say you think about my family, what exactly do you wonder about? Are you afraid of what I may ask you at some point—like the night you came into my house—or are you hoping I ask you about those details?

You mention you owe me everything I've asked for and more—do you think it's even possible to pay back for what you've done and how you've affected my life? Our criminal justice system thinks it's prison, but I wonder otherwise. What do you think of restorative justice or whatever this can be categorized as? Have you watched people in prison go through this process before?

I too feel that this process is so compelling I must see it through, whatever that looks like and on whatever timeline that it takes. Thank you for acknowledging the courage it has taken to do this. I hope that this ongoing discussion reveals more about who I am. I feel more at peace than I had previous to contacting you. This feels like an integral part of moving toward further peace. So thank you for contributing to that.

Carys

"Carys, make sure Mom gets the prettiest dress in the store for our dinner on Friday," her father tells her.

When she and her mother go shopping, they enter a vintage second-hand store. She stares at all the fabrics and colours that defined earlier generations. Her mother pulls silly-looking dresses off the rack to tease her; they remind her mother of the ones she sewed in the sixties, for high school and college celebrations.

She pictures the dress her mother made for a high school cheer-leading competition: a short, A-line baby doll made of rayon, with a swirling bright pink and orange geometric pattern, as though straight out of a Mary Quant catalogue.

Her mother wore it for the 1960s-themed party her parents recently hosted at their house. They rented black lights and a disco ball, and they played Motown hits all night long. She stayed up late to watch the adults dance. While her mother got ready, she said she was applying her mascara "like Twiggy."

Her mother selects a few dresses and walks to the change room, where she tries them on.

"That one," she says to her mother when she appears from behind the curtain.

Her mother wears a black sleeveless teacup dress that goes down over her knees. Satin ribbon finishes the seams and defines the waistline that rests at her ribs. The precisely pleated chiffon streams from her waist and sways with her movements.

She approaches her mother and feels the fabric run through her fingers.

"Yes, this is it," her mother says.

MEDICINE
FOR THE SOUL

Like clockwork, the next letter came to my office within a couple of weeks of sending him mine. I slid the fax into my bag and at the end of the work day, I drove to the same restaurant, sat down in a booth and, after ordering some fries, started reading.

September 22, 2011

Carys

First off I would like to thank you for sharing with me about your profession. I feel you when you tell me that these kids need some kind of guidance from their dejected lives. In my experiences with social workers guidance counsellors group homes projecting their own beliefs morals and inadequacies on to these kids pushes them further into their own oblivious worlds. I have always thought that some of these kids have violence engraved into their everyday lives and this is all they know. So with these thoughts and feelings of being no good they seek out others they have things in common with. The last thing they want to hear is views on how they should be. Instead the focus should be on what they want out of life and try to plant a seed that whatever it is they are into, they do it to the best of their ability. If there is a kid that is very much into sports and the group home goes and puts him on a soccer team, with out even asking him how do you think he'll do? What if he wants to play hockey? This is exactly what happened with me, I had no interest in playing soccer but was forced to do it regardless. They need to find out what makes these kids tick.

My philosophy exactly, I thought, recalling the teenage boy who'd recently taught me what fan fiction was and the teenage girl with dreams of being a fashion designer. I'd assigned her homework, which included wearing something cool that reflected her style to our next session. I'll always remember the bright yellow slipper shoes she proudly wore into the counselling room, wanting me to notice.

I don't want you to think that I am attacking you and your profession. I have been in every one of those kids' shoes in one way or the other. But being in their shoes doesn't make me an expert on why they do what they do. You have an opportunity here to make life better, not for all but absolutely for some. The task that you have taken on is very time consuming and you will experience failure, hopelessness and melancholy at times. What you do with those feelings is a challenge.

I had invited his reflections about my work by sharing details with him, but I felt uncomfortable, almost patronized: *you will experience failure.* I wanted to hear his world view, but when he spoke directly to me as though educating me on my profession, I felt anger. *You will. You do.* I furrowed my eyebrows, pushed my lips to the side.

I have a lot of trepidation about what I will do when I get out. I'm 41 right now and I have nothing to show for it so I know that financially it will be a struggle. Even though I have not squandered my stay here who will hire a murderer. I would like to think that I will be ok if I work hard at whatever I end up doing. I have a lot of different qualifications, which may help but I'm not expecting handouts from the government. My family lives in a small town but if I move there people will find out who I am as I have to report to the police everywhere I go.

This serves up a whole other dilemma for my family. I know that they are doing very well with what they have. Insert a murderer in the mix wouldn't likely go over so well with the community. Even though they tell me that I could move to the nearest city that has a halfway house so that they could visit me on weekends. I want to have my own family one day, I have a lot to offer. I want to find someone that will look past my idiosyncracies and past transgressions and love me for who I am today. Tall order or what?

When you ask me if I can pay you back for the death of your father, absolutely not, there is nothing I can do to change what happened that night. Hopefully I can honour his life by making the most out of mine. If this is part of the journey then I welcome it. You reached out to me for a reason what you expect from me might not be what you need, but this is a great opportunity to find out. I was surprised and apprehensive when you first contacted me. Now I feel that you can look at this as medicine for the soul. I know that the couple of letters you have written me, gave me the comfort to tell you everything you want to know. So if you want to know something about why I did what I did, then I will try and share.

I appreciated these words, words I had hoped he'd share on his own. I, too, was beginning to view this as medicine for the soul.

> When my grandfather was killed in front of my mother, she had never dealt with it. Until recently, I was thinking to myself this is why my childhood was the way it was, did this deep sorrow she held in all these years somehow have some effect on the way we were brought up. Should I blame my grandfather for the way I turned out? Let me explain the last statement to you. I don't know the exact night this happened to her because I didn't have the foresight to ask her. My grandfather had gotten it in his mind to murder everyone in the home one night; got himself some coal oil poured it all around the house and proceeded to light the house on fire. He was then confronted by my great uncle and a struggle had ensued. My grandfather was stabbed and he died from the wounds.

I pushed my hand into my chest and felt my breath getting deeper. *My grandfather was stabbed and he died from the wounds.*

> This took place in front of my mother, my uncle and my other aunt. How does one go through life not dealing with such tragedy? Or maybe she dealt with it the only way she knew how. Did this have some kind of ripple effect or was what I did to your family all me.

I soaked up the pain.

> I don't know anybody else that is going through this process. So I can't comment on it. I have found that worrying about others

in here and confiding in others about your personal business can only lead to trouble. When you have been here for as long as I have you tend to try and keep your life as private as possible. The reason for that is it gives people ammunition against you if you ever have a falling out with them. They then take what ever info they have and use it to harm you any way they can.

So enough about me, let's talk about you. Do your siblings know that you are talking with me if so how do they feel about it? Do you have anybody in your life that you share this experience with beside me? I'm just curious about how they perceive this connection. What does your other brother and sisters do, how do they cope do you talk with them. If you feel that these questions are to forward please feel free to let me know.

You haven't really set any boundaries as to what we can ask each other, so I will ask what is on my mind. What do you expect out of me? What can I tell you that can help you with those oppressed feeling you have about your profession?

Just as quickly as I'd been brought in to pain, I was brought out by disgust. *Oppressed feelings*. What does that even mean? And no, I don't need your help. Thank you. Very. Much.

This country is building more prisons to lock up the kids that you are trying to help keep free. This country is becoming a police state. The rich get richer the middle and poor become homeless and are starting to fight back. What can we do as a society to rectify the situation? Maybe you need to just keep doing what you're doing and hope that you can at the very least change someone's life for the better. Look how you have me thinking about things that I normally don't think about. This has been such a good experience for me that I wouldn't know how to greet you if I met you in person, do I acknowledge you with a head nod do I stand and give you a hand shake or maybe a hug? How would you like me to greet you if we meet? After being so disconnected with the world some of my social concepts have fallen at the waist side.

So until we talk again take care in knowing that you have made my day. If there is something that you would like to hear you have to be forthright in saying so.

Thank you.

Sheldon

The clatter of the restaurant brought me back to my surroundings. I picked a fry off my plate and noticed it had become cold. I wanted to write back immediately, ask him questions, respond to his ideas, tell him how his story resonated with me, and challenge his assumptions while ignoring some things entirely. There were hundreds of tangents I could take. Instead, I folded the letter in half, leaned back into my booth, and ordered more fries.

I t's time for you to go upstairs," her father informs her mother.

Her sisters and brother and she stand ready in the kitchen, waiting for further instruction. Together, they prepare marinated flank steak, corn on the cob, and french fries from scratch, her parents' favourite dishes. Her father helps his children push the potato through the french fry cutter, its cast-iron weight heavy on the floor. The windows and sliding glass door steam up from the deep-fryer's heat. They set the table with the corkboard placemats adorned with sketches of scenes from Durham, in the UK—which inspire their mother to tell them stories about her time there at college—and with the maroon- and gold-edged china that only comes out for Christmas dinners. While they adhere short birthday cake candles to the table with sticky tack, their father takes a knife from its block and carves the steak into thin strips, revealing their pink centres.

"Go get your mom," he tells them.

They rush to her room, excited to escort her down the stairs. She looks beautiful in her new dress. They ready themselves to serve as he plates the food. While their parents eat in the kitchen, they eat downstairs and play.

After they finish dinner, their father positions all of them around their mother, who sits at the kitchen table. He grabs his camera.

She stands behind her mother, with her new pixie cut, wearing a black T-shirt tucked into a pink and green floral cotton knee-length skirt. She smiles the smile she has inherited from her parents.

Her mother, sitting proud at the table, her hair lifted into a bun, smiles as though she could not be happier and more in love with her family.

"Everyone ready?" he asks.

They shift in their places.

"On the count of three. One, two, three. Smile." The shutter opens and closes.

It is the last photograph he will take.

PART THREE

IN IRONS

When the bow of a sailboat is headed into the wind and the
boat has stalled and is unable to maneuver.

—Sailing Terms, NauticEd

RESIGNED

Perhaps I'd taken on too much that fall. Too many roles and responsibilities, with little breathing room. One night after a terrible evening meeting with my client's foster family, I stood paralyzed in the toiletries aisle of the local grocery store.

Fluorescent lights assaulted my tired eyes. I needed toothpaste, but for the life of me I was incapable of making a decision. I looked around, thankful no one could see my face as tears built up in my eyes. *What am I doing?* I shivered, my thoughts spiralling through a series of disappointments at work.

Years before, I interviewed for a youth outreach counsellor job.

"I think you'd be a good fit," my soon-to-be supervisor said. She was the first of five supervisors in a little over three years, a turnover I hadn't known then is typical in the social services field.

"I'm not into diagnosing youth," I said. "In my master's internship, I was informed that I have to diagnose. For youth to get access to our service."

"We're the outreach program. I want you to develop relationships with them, engage them in service. You don't have to diagnose," she replied.

I weighed the pros and cons. Eventually, I decided that I would take the job to learn the language of the most influential social services organization in the province. I would familiarize myself with the system that attempts and fails to respond to vulnerable and marginalized young people and their families. I would learn its language to see how I could change it. Once I learned what I needed to know, I reasoned, I would leave.

"Can we do a satisfaction survey to see how the social workers are finding this mental-health consultation role?" I asked my second supervisor. When she agreed, I created a questionnaire, and the responses showed evidence that the service was beneficial—helping the child protection social workers learn how mental health issues present themselves in their clients' lives—but the service was eventually cut. No more specialized roles, the leadership said.

"We need a volunteer for the school consultant position." Before my third supervisor had finished describing the role—consulting with teachers and youth workers on mental health issues in an alternative-education classroom in an inner-city school—my hand went up. No one else seemed to want the position.

"I don't think he's appropriate for services. I don't think he even comprehends what I'm saying," I said to my fourth supervisor after a thorough assessment of a client and family.

She replied, "Just do a round of cognitive behavioural therapy and then close."

I wanted to yell at her, "This family needs a physician and a dentist, a nutritionist, someone to help them with literacy, someone to help them communicate with their kids' school, to fill out forms for assistance. They don't need counselling!"

But by then, I figured no one was really listening, so I'd just do it anyway.

Bless my fifth supervisor, who supported my secondment to the practice analyst role.

"We just track numbers of families pushed through the system.

We don't even track outcomes of the services we provide. How do we know if we're even effective?" I ranted to her while she simply nodded. But I saw that even she—energetic, charismatic, and respectful of the kids—couldn't do much to change it.

A few hours before I found myself at the grocery store, I was sitting on the basement floor in the house of my client's foster family.

"He's being manipulative," the foster mother said in front of my client, berating him for separately asking permission from both foster parents to go to the school dance.

"He doesn't know your house rules yet. He's never had two parents at one time before. He just wants to go to a grade eight dance," I said in return.

"No. I won't allow it," she said. She looked down at him and me sitting next to each other on the floor from where she sat on the only chair in the room. *Fitting,* I thought.

"I told him to ask you. This isn't his fault. It's mine," I said. "This is the most pro-social thing he's done since I've met him. He wants to go to a dance." Aware of my client sitting just a few feet away, his head hanging low, my nerves began to take hold, a balance to the fear induced by her scowl.

"No," she repeated.

My client got up, ran to the bathroom, and locked himself inside.

"I'll leave. You can talk to him," she said, as though I was her servant and we weren't in this together.

She walked confidently out of the room and up the stairs, like she had made her power known, informed us who was in charge.

"I'm so sorry," I said to my client through the bathroom door. "This is my fault. This isn't your fault." Tears ran down my face. "I'm so sorry," I said again. I could hear him crying.

Now, I stared at some fixed point between me and the rows of toothpaste. *What exactly was I doing with my life?*

The glaring question was why I had become accustomed to chaos and crisis, exhausted by the futility of my role and the system I found myself in. While I had no idea how to answer this, I knew it was the question I was supposed to be asking myself.

I did the only thing I knew to disrupt what was happening.

I resigned from the Ministry.

As the year closed and a new one began, I settled into an uncertain future. In the first month, I couldn't help but notice that I visited friends more often than I had in the previous twelve months. I read more and wrote more. I continued to learn to cook, hung out in coffee shops, and attended even more arts and culture events in the city, wondering all the while what my future would hold.

"Oh my god, what am I going to do?" I said to Shannon, softly bouncing her six-month-old daughter on my lap and making humming noises above her head.

"Exactly what you're doing," she said as she fixed lunch in the kitchen. "Look at her grin," she pointed to the baby's face, which I couldn't see below me, but I heard her giggle.

Shannon left the kitchen and came into the living room, changing the topic. "Do you think he's being changed by this?"

"That's what the workers say, that he's acting differently."

"I think you're offering him something he's never experienced before."

"Yeah," I said. "Maybe."

Before bedtime, four children gather on their parents' bed: one is underneath the blankets, one sits cross-legged in the middle of the bed, one lays on her back, and one hangs off the end, head resting on the trunk at the foot of the bed.

"Where should we go for a family trip?" their father asks them. Their mother smiles, knowing he is teasing them, that they have already made plans.

"What about Disneyland?" he asks.

Their eyes widen, they jump up from their resting positions and shout with delight. He grins.

Some of the kids are more daredevil than the others, but they all enjoy roller coasters and how their parents never seem to tire.

Their father loves telling them adventure stories: his own about being dropped from a helicopter to ski on a mountaintop in British Columbia or about sailing across the Pacific Ocean in his twenties, and the ones he plans each year for them, such as where the family may live after he finishes his residency.

"That's it. It's decided. We're going to Disneyland," he confirms.

They all go to bed, trying their best to get to sleep after the excitement of the news.

Six hours later, they will wake up to the noise of their mother's screams and the sight of blood covering the walls and their father collapsed on the front steps, their lives changed forever.

MY FATHER

11

riving home from Shannon's, I felt upset that Sheldon kept writing about himself and hardly referred to my father. I had gently eased us into a conversation, to ensure it was safe. And now I wanted to write about my father. I never knew exactly what I wanted to say, until I opened my computer and began typing.

January 8, 2012

Sheldon,

It has been a while since I've written to you, which you're obviously aware. Many events conspired this fall that have required my energy, my time, my ability to be fully present.

I re-read your letter and want to respond to a few things you mention.

You say that you can honour my dad's life by making the most of yours and I really appreciate that. But I don't believe you can do this until you know my father. The thousands of people who showed up to his memorial service will each have a different way to describe who my dad was and the pain they've endured. I feel it's a good time to explain a little of who he was and who he continues to be.

My dad is the eldest of five children. He grew up in and around BC. He was always into trying new things artistically, physically, always challenging himself. In his twenties he sailed around the world on his sailboat. I grew up with this same sailboat, spending summers on it. We sailed around the Sunshine Coast in BC. I've only travelled the world a bit but I truly think it's the most beautiful place in the world. He liked to ski, including dangerous helicopter skiing, getting dropped off on a mountain with his friends. He, being a physician, would always be the guy to stitch up his friends' minor cuts when doing these dangerous things. He had a family medical practice with his dad in Vancouver. His patients loved him. He delivered hundreds of babies. He was very good at a party. The life of the party. In every conversation he had with people—his patients, his colleagues, his family—he'd make you feel like the most important person in the room. He made violins from scratch. He joined a fiddler's musical group in Calgary. He loved to watch us practice musical instruments, or me when I used to sing. He made us tree forts and other crazy contraptions in our back yard. He built houses. He loved my mother and this—witnessing this kindness, respect, and love—made me have faith that kids can have a good picture of good relationships of the utmost respect, so that they can create the same thing one day. He loved us—he had a special connection with each of his children. He had traditions with each of us that were based on each of our own interests. He always wanted us to be learning. And he was silly with us. He really knew how to have fun, not a quality many people possess. He thought we were pretty cool—and I like it when any adult thinks kids are cool, because I think it makes them feel confident when trying to

figure out this crazy, confusing world that we all live in. When
he was in his early forties he took a leap of faith and went back
to school to specialize as an orthopedic surgeon. He used to
study long hours and spend an incredible amount of time at
university and Foothills Hospital. I remember this to be the
most incredible strength—that you could change mid-life, do
what you were most interested in even after so many people
wondered why he would leave a good medical practice, risk
everything financially and socially, an established life. I think
that when he would have graduated, he planned on creating a
clinic specializing in sports medicine. I continue a relationship
with him to this day, and I continually try to find new ways to
uphold his life and let his influence on my life take new and
creative paths.

Writing of family, I should respond to your question about
the rest of my family. There just hasn't been a good time to
inform my immediate family that I'm writing to you. I have
no doubt I'll inform them at some point. I am able to share
this process with a few of my close friends because they have
a vested interest in my well-being first and foremost and are
not connected to you in the same way as my family is. I don't
know how my family would perceive the connection we now
have. I'll find out soon enough, but not yet.

You ask about my siblings. Other than to say I adore my
family, I do not feel it is right or appropriate for me to share
anything about them, as that's not my right to share. I will
share aspects of me with you, as I feel comfortable and as I
feel appropriate, but these are my stories. But let me tell you,
it has been a difficult road for each of us, and continues to be.
The best version of coping I've come up with is to continue a

relationship with my dad, past death, and to be myself the best I can. People (mostly psychologists, etc.) try to get people back to 'normal' as though nothing happened. But I strongly disagree with these approaches. I believe that how you crashed into my life that night will always exist and it's up to me to make the best of that, to learn something, to be a better person because of it, to be responsible for contributing to the world instead of destroying it. That is my approach to coping.

You say that I haven't set any boundaries. I feel that the tone and pacing of our letters is a boundary in and of itself. But yes, feel free to ask what you want to ask. If you feel it's appropriate to ask and I feel comfortable to respond, then that's the boundary. I could ask you a million things—about you, about that night, about details—but I haven't because I only ask things that feel right in that moment. I have no interest in the gory details of death, but perhaps at some point I will ask you those types of questions.

I'll tell you one thing though, I really don't want my feelings of my profession to come across as 'oppressed,' as you reflect. I know I'm the minority about how I feel about well-being, justice, and care. And I'm okay with that. I bet we could have quite a good conversation about the current Canadian policies of the hardcore right-wing conservatives wanting to build prisons instead of helping families, wanting to indirectly support guns being distributed instead of fund early childhood education, etc. I'd welcome your opinions. And I'd welcome being challenged on mine. Yes, that politician has a surprising amount of power in his/her ability to create a policy that impacts my life and yours. But here we are, in our positions in society. And that is that.

I'm really struggling, philosophically/politically, with how we (as a society, you included) should have responded to you (as an individual) before you killed my dad. People spend their entire professional careers (criminal justice, police, rehabilitation) trying to figure out how to care for people who have been disadvantaged, trying to alter people's life trajectories to not lead to destructive behaviour, trying to balance individual rights and freedoms with the rights of community. As you can probably tell through my writing to you, I doubt the current crime & punishment philosophy of the day/past few centuries does much to deal with the injustice that has happened. This model seems to privilege those who think that 25 years is a good amount of time and a good response to someone responsible for killing someone. But all the 25 years seems to do is take you out of society, keeping you from doing the same thing to another member of society with the faint hope of you not doing it again once you leave prison. And during this time, it's up to me, as a so-called victim (of your acts) to contact you to engage in something other than what is socially accepted. Talk about being a minority in a world of people who wish punishment in response to crime. What am I to do with this option? Take the rage in me and take it out on you? I could do that. And I'm sure our current society would accept that as okay (even if I know it's not). I could 'forgive,' whatever on earth that even means these days. I could pretend you don't exist, pretend that my dad just died out of nowhere (this seems to be society's way of doing things). But no, I'm stuck in your life and you're stuck in mine, for better or for worse. And if I were to engage you about these matters in a conversation, as we're doing slowly but surely, then maybe that would somehow contribute to righting the wrong that you did.

I need to say that I do not believe you are 100% responsible for the injustice you brought into my home that evening. I will never understand why you chose to actually kill him, but I can certainly understand how the circumstance availed itself to you, given the circumstances you've endured in your life. Aligned to this, I do not believe I am 100% responsible for the life that I am leading today. I was given caring, competent, intelligent parents. I was given an extended family who has the best intentions for me and my life. I was given access to education. I had access to people who do not engage in unjust acts. I was given the privilege of financial security, even though your act caused that aspect of my life to be significantly disrupted for some time. I had the privilege of living in a safe community. And because I have these lovely things in my life, I feel that has made me able to make choices. If these circumstances did not exist, I'm not sure what choices I'd make. I don't wish to put us on the opposite sides of the spectrum of good and bad choices, good and bad lives, good and bad people, but I certainly wish to express that neither of us is 100% responsible for our successes or failures.

With all of that said, who chooses to kill someone? Fine, enter my home, steal what you want, terrify us to the core of our being, but to kill someone, to end a life? What made it an option for you to do such a horrible act? Do you think about that?

Me, I'll spend my entire life trying to figure out why, despite all the horrible acts that you've experienced, you took the selfish privilege in that moment to consider your life more important than my father's; why you took the audacious power, why, in that moment, you opened that kitchen drawer to find a knife; why you walked up those stairs knowing it's a family home and not an abandoned industrial building; why you met body to body with my father—one of the most creative, strong, genuine, caring, intelligent, and still flawed people I'll ever know in my life—and inflicted absolute violent pain in him while he was attempting to protect the most important people in his life; why instead of running away, instead of having a lesser violent conflict, you decided to kill him. If you can explain that to me, then go right ahead.

Oh, and to respond to your last questions, don't worry about how to greet me. I'd like you to look me in the eyes. And I'd like you to shake my hand. But we'll figure that out later. Right now, I'd like to continue this conversation.

Thank you,

Carys

She awakens to her mother's screams. It is dark. She does not know the time. She fumbles her way out of her bed to the hallway, looks down the stairs. Blood covers the rough walls where the wallpaper was recently removed, and it is soaked into the cream shag carpet. She can smell it.

"Carys, call 9-1-1!" her mother yells from the floor below.

She returns to her room, finds her phone near her bed. It was a gift to her on her birthday. She lifts the receiver and places it close to her ear, worrying that her cheek will depress the switch. She dials 9-1-1 on the phone's piano-shaped keys.

The emergency responder repeatedly asks, "How old is your dad?" and "How old are you?" and doesn't let her leave the phone.

"He's forty-four years old, I think. I'm eleven years old. He's hurt. There's blood everywhere."

After the ambulance arrives, her neighbour takes her and her siblings next door. As they walk, she feels the moist grass beneath her toes. She and her siblings sit on blankets in the playroom. Her neighbours return upstairs to their sleeping sons and newborn.

She can't fall asleep. Feeling the tingling rise of nausea in her throat, she walks to the bathroom and sits in the corner with her back against the wall. She stretches her nightgown over her toes, holds her knees close to her chest, and shivers, alone.

12
HIS STORY

*H*e *does write a bit about the actual crime, so she may want a heads-up about that,* Jennifer wrote on the fax cover page. I sat in the boardroom at the CJI offices, where I hadn't been in some time. As I read her note, I braced myself.

"You've read this, right?" I asked, after seeing the gentle warning.

"Yes," Sandi confirmed. Dave nodded.

> January 16, 2012
>
> Carys,
>
> Hi thank you for responding to my questions you are very thorough in your responses. I am a little taken aback from the description of your father and understand how painful his loss was to you and your family. I had no idea about his life's accomplishments.

I paused and wondered, *What do you mean you didn't have any idea?*

> How does someone so insignificant respond to such a poignant and influential response? I am stumped for words. I certainly envy the fact that you and your father shared such a profound

bond. I had no such bond with any one of my parents. I can't believe this was my fault, or maybe it was. I still haven't dealt with that aspect of my life. You asked me what I will do with myself when I get out. I have close to a thousand dollars saved right now. By the time I get out I hopefully will incur some financial assistance to help gets started. With the skills that I have I could probably get a job at a warehouse. Maybe frame homes or renovate homes but I will take whatever I can get.

I know that every day will be a struggle for me, like I've said before I will always be a murderer and will be ostracized for the most part. So in the grand scheme of things I'm basically set up for failure. How does one overcome such obstacles? Financial freedom would help but I would have to win the lottery. So I guess I will have to strive and struggle to make the best out of this bad situation that I have gotten myself into. I really don't intend on getting a wife or kids for that matter so I will only have myself to support. I would like to find love but who in their right mind would fall in love with a murderer. How would I rate my successes in life well? It will be measured on if I can maintain my sobriety and the building of friendships, something that I really have a hard time achieving because of my past. This is why that would be a significant achievement. I do not have the right to burden my family with my presence. They have their lives, and for me to insert myself into the mix would be selfish and inconsiderate. I suspect that I will live a lonely existence until I die, but I'm hoping and striving to not let that happen.

You asked me if I reflect on what I did to your father, if you only new. First off I would like to tell you, no matter what you think you know, no matter what you have heard. I did not intend to kill your father I tried to run away when I heard him yell.

But didn't they prove he went toward the noise? I thought.

He caught me at the bottom of the stairs and started to strike me in the back of the head. I in no way blame him for protecting his family the way he did. I did not have a chance to stand in front of him and tell him that I have a knife and to back off.

But couldn't he have dropped the knife? I wondered.

He was on my back when I had blindly swung the knife back and struck him in the chest he still didn't stop so I then struck him again in the ribs when he didn't fall after that blow I then bent over to avoid more of his blows and struck him again in the shin, at which time the knife had broke and fell to the ground, as did your father. I then ran out the front door and made my way over to the stadium. There I called a cab, gave him my name not knowing the damage I had done, and went home. I can tell you that I did pray to god to not let your father die that night from my terrible deed but it wasn't to be, this is how I lost my faith in god. After I had found out what I had done I cried for about three hours. Then all I could do is sit and wait for the police to come.

Was that all that you could do? I interjected, questioning the way he was telling his story, how he was explaining the horrible things he had done.

To be known as the man that took your father's life was devastating for me, not to mention how horrible it was for you and your family.

The prosecutor offered me twelve years to plead guilty. I did not want to be a murderer I didn't want to be the guy that took someone else's life. So I took the advice of my lawyer and told them not guilty. Then I had to come up with viable defence. This is a whole other story at which I will not get into at the moment. You see, by me telling you what happened that night kind of diminishes the concept of the authorities. This is of no consequence to me. I had told you before that I will not try and sugar coat the truth with you. The fact that your father maybe thought that he was protecting you guys from danger was commendable. The price he paid in doing so was inexcusable, and unforgivable. What was I thinking about at the time was how did I get to this point in my life. What kind of monetary gain can I leave with to get through to my next couple of days? The time I had to get in and out of your home was cut short by the noise I heard upstairs. Upon closer examination I had found out that there were people there and when I reached the doorway of your father's bedroom he awoke we saw each other he yelled, I ran.

I didn't understand. He didn't have to walk up to my parents' room. He had to have known people were in the house. There were two cars. The house was messy, lived in. There were people sleeping in the bedrooms of the windows he'd peered into before breaking in.

When I think about the opportunity I had to leave and didn't, this becomes a problem for me. Why didn't I leave when I heard that noise? Why did I decided to go and find out where that noise came from? These are questions that I can't answer because I have no answer for them. Can I blame drugs and alcohol? Or was it that I stopped caring about life in general. I'm so sorry Carys I have no answers for the choices I made that night.

I had up until this time broke into garages and taken tools I don't know what possessed me to go into your home that night. I probably thought that I could be descreet enough to not get caught. All I know is that I will never be thrust into that situation no matter what happens to me in life. There are ways to deal with my addictions and emotions today. That I did not know about at the time. I will always have positive people in my life that I can turn to in case I am having a hard time coping. I know that there will be a lot scrutinizing on the part of parole people. They are here to help me as I become part of society once again. Maybe I'll try to get a student loan I wouldn't mind becoming an addictions counsellor I have managed to guide a lot of people in the right direction and I know first hand what it can do to an individual. I don't practice AA theology I find the religious aspects undermine the purpose of why they are there. There are other ways to deal with those problems other than being thrust into a cult. I did have the privilege of giving these meetings a try. I found that they depressed me more than when I went in and that having my life put on display made me very uncomfortable. I sought out private therapy and found that this was much more beneficial for me. Getting in touch with the emotional side of why you feel the way you feel is much more beneficial. I have found my niche in life and think that I have a lot to offer people. Getting the opportunity to do so is the problem. Should I struggle and strive to be a counsellor with no one to counsel. Sit in an empty office because people will eventually find out what I did, murder a man. What then do I tell them yes, I did and if you don't stop using drugs this could happen to you do I become a poster boy for drug addiction? Maybe I should just accept my punishment and spend my life in prison. The food is pretty good I have free cable and I don't have bills to pay I don't have to work hard to survive. Sure I'm not out in the community but what does the community have that I need?

I will never forget the things that I have done, the pain that I have caused. But it would be a waste if I don't try and take this opportunity and try to help others as well. Where to start this journey I hope will reveal itself in time.

I would like to say that writing to you and sharing these thoughts with you help me understand more about you and myself. I have until recently never thought about the existence of the emotional impact I had on your life. You make me want to do good things with my life, because if I don't, I will be letting you down and that is the last thing I want to do. When the opportunity does come that I do have a chance to change a life, you have my solemn vow that I will try diligently to do so, starting with my own. Like I said before, it won't come easy for me but after I finally achieve some kind of existence, I hope to still be in contact with you. Keeping in touch with you is something that I will not take lightly. This is not to ease your worries that I may commit another crime this is because you have taken the opportunity to get to know what makes me tick. Like you said before, you could just bash me belittle my existence and get on with your life. By acknowledging me and accepting me into your life shows that you care about what happens to

me. Or are you making sure that I don't commit another crime.
What can I tell you to ease your mind? You seem to have it in
your mind that I wanted to kill your father. I did not want to
kill anybody I didn't know he was your father I didn't know
that he was your mother's husband your grandmother's son
your uncle's brother I had no idea who he was what he did all
I knew at the time is that I needed to get away by any means
necessary. What possessed me to use a knife? This was only
to be a show of force not a weapon of death. Fear is a very
complex emotion. With the addition of drugs and the mindset
I was in, the seconds it took to commit this horrendous act
was a vicious cocktail that should never have been consumed.
I would like you to know that even though I have committed
such a crime does not mean that this defines who I am. Maybe
one day you will see that I was a young, thoughtless, desperate
kid that made terrible choices in life because he didn't have
many other choices to grab on to.

We as a society need to figure out what is criminal and
what is just circumstance. But then how do you deal with the
victims what kind of compensation do they get. Are we so
barbaric that we can't figure out a happy medium? This cycle
that we have created for ourselves will only lead to chaos this
country will have everybody locked up for one reason or another.
There will always be injustice in this world for both victim and
perpetrators. Prevention is the key having guidance places to
turn to and not be turned away. Giving people the opportunities
that the privileged have would be great. How to achieve free
healthcare. How to achieve free schooling. Having a roof over
your head, breaking the cycles of our past would be a good
start. Maybe communism, true communism wasn't a bad idea,

who am I kidding freedom of choice is a good thing. Anyway, on that note I will be sending this off to you and I hope I have kindly enough shed some light on where my mind is at today.

Thank you for writing.

Sheldon

Two phrases looped in my mind. *I had no idea who he was,* and *I have never thought about the existence of the emotional impact I had on your life.* I sat staring, my hand covering my mouth, while Dave and Sandi sat silently across from me. He didn't know anything about my dad until now. He hadn't thought about the emotional impact on me until now. Until now. What, then, had he been doing these past twenty years?

I looked up. "You know," I began, "he lied about it all."

He blamed his friend, some guy he'd been breaking into garages with. I always wondered why he lied when the evidence was so clear. There was only one set of footprints around the house. There was only one set of glove prints on the windows. There was only one voice heard when we all awoke. His hand was cut from the knife's force; so too was the glove found with him. The knife was left behind, broken in two from the third stab to my father's body. Chest. Shoulder. Shin. The cab driver who picked Sheldon up at the strip mall a few blocks from our house remembered his name and remembered the house where he dropped him off.

But he continued to lie for fifteen years more, even after the trial and appeal. Perhaps it wasn't the lying that was so awful but what he trying to cover up. It wasn't the absurdity of the lie that was unnerving but his lack of accountability for what he'd done. Stupid, offensive, insidiously unnerving to swear before the lawyers, jury, my father's family, and my mother under oath that he hadn't done what he was accused of.

"He had an appeal a year or two after the trial," I explained to

Dave and Sandi. "But the jurors hadn't believed his story the first time around. And the appeal judge stuck with the original sentence. They couldn't prove he came to our house on purpose, with the intent to kill. Second-degree murder with a first-degree sentence. Life in prison. Chance for parole at twenty-five years."

As a child during the appeal, I didn't understand why someone could be allowed to actively seek, and be given, another chance to lie. I wanted to know why someone would have the nerve to offend the courts, the community, me, and, most importantly, my father.

I wanted to say, *Tell me why you didn't give yourself up to the police.* His crime wasn't just the murder. *Understand the consequences of your decisions*, I wanted to tell him. Understand the whole of the crime, not just the split-second act of stabbing my father to death. Understand my needs, as one of your hundreds of victims.

Instead of being able to live my life as I wished, I had to wrestle with pain, confusion, and unanswered questions. Now it was my task to figure out how to say this and ensure he was listening.

After her father dies, they visit Vancouver for two weeks, where they stay at her grandparents' house to spend time with her mother's family and her parents' friends while planning the memorial service.

She and her siblings sit in the living room watching television. She misses her school friends in Calgary and wonders what they are doing. She moves over to the stairs and sits, listening for noise from her mother's room. She wants to be near her.

"Don't bother your mother, dear," her grandmother says when she sees her slowly walking up the stairs. She wants to cry but holds her breath, stops, walks down a few stairs, and stands at the doorway to the living room. After her grandmother returns to the kitchen, she quickly sneaks upstairs, slowly opens the door, and sees her mother lying on the bed, awake.

"Come here," her mother says and makes room for her on the bed.

Her mother calls it a memorial service, not a funeral, and when she asks why, her mother tells her it is because they will all gather to celebrate her father's life. Her aunts take them shopping and she gets a maroon-coloured, floral-patterned dress for the service.

When she arrives at the yacht club near Jericho Beach, she remembers coming here each summer to load and unload *Tangerine* for their summer trips. She liked to try to fit as much as possible into the wheelbarrow and remembers how it bounced as her parents wheeled it up the steep ramp and along the series of docks that led to the boat.

She notices everyone is dressed up. Not in black, as is typically worn at a funeral, but in many colours. The sun shines brightly, and she and her cousins run around the lawn that looks out on the marina and beyond to English Bay, while the adults gather inside getting ready for the speeches.

Years later, her mother tells her that at the same time they gathered to celebrate the life of her father, so too did a group of people in Calgary: hundreds of neighbours, colleagues, patients, and friends.

SEPTEMBER 16, 1992

As I drove away from the CJI office, the horizon of farmland, lampposts, and dilapidated houses along my route through the Fraser Valley blended into one another. My own images of those early hours came back to me, recalled by Sheldon's account of that night.

I hovered above the scenes, wanting to lunge into the darkness of that early morning, to sit in front of my younger self, look deeply into her eyes, and tell her she's going to be okay. I wanted to leap across the space between us to hug her. I couldn't, though, not able to cross the space and time that separates us.

While my siblings lay in the playroom of our neighbours' house, I hugged my legs and stared at the bathroom floor. *What just happened to my family?* I had watched the pieces of my life explode, shattering the world I knew. All of what I contained inside me was expelled into time and space, leaving me empty and bereft, as if the tiny world I had known had just expanded so wide I was alone in its aftermath, trembling from the shock of a world disrupted. Alone, now, with so much more to know.

I rejoined my siblings in the playroom. While I'd been on the phone with emergency services, they had been next to my father, who was lying on the concrete front path while our neighbours pressed their night clothes against his wounds.

We spoke to each other optimistically. "Maybe he'll be like the guy on TV," referring to the crime drama we had taken up, where the injured victim always survives.

My mother returned from the hospital. I don't remember how she told us, what words she used to inform us that our lives had changed forever, but while she stood alongside my favourite family friend, I remember watching her face, her hunched body looking smaller than usual in her familiar colourful, baggy jacket.

My sister asked, "But who will walk us down the aisle?"

Family from Vancouver arrived at the house. Aunts. Uncles. Grandmothers. Grandfathers. Then came neighbours, friends' parents, and school staff. Someone patted me on the shoulder.

Because we weren't allowed back in our house, my aunts replaced our clothing, forgetting to pick up socks. I didn't like the sweaty feeling and rough fabric of the new slip-on sneakers against my bare skin.

The window curtains were closed, but I snuck looks outside to where reporters stood waiting alongside the crime scene tape surrounding our lawn. I stood motionless, like life had been hollowed out. It was the only home I'd known since I was six years old, in a neighbourhood where I babysat next door and walked to the school around the corner with my friends, picking up schoolmates along the way. I remember that home as my childhood. But early that morning, I felt something leave, even though I didn't know exactly what it was. I felt it leave my body, go to some unknown place, to where there was a strong chance it might not be recovered.

Each night a pill was placed underneath our tongues. We slept on mattresses pushed together in my neighbour's basement: aunt, child, aunt, child, mother, child, grandmother, child, aunt. Days were filled with the aftermath of the crime: police interviews, watching the news reports on television from a bed in our friends' home down the street from ours, and waiting for the police to find the killer.

At the funeral home before Dad was cremated, I stood next to his body, which lay on the table in the plain beige room. My mother, siblings, grandmother, and aunts stood nearby. I wondered where the wounds were, where he had been hurt. He looked the same, but not like himself. I could no longer hear his kind, playful voice. The big smile that always crossed his face, the smile I had inherited, was gone. All the life was gone. I didn't touch him. I began to wail uncontrollably. My aunt took me to the chairs along one wall of the small room and told me to breathe slowly, deeply, as she placed her hand on my back.

I looked up from my hunched position, toward my dad.

He was gone.

She positions herself on the basement stairs, leaning against the wall with the shag carpeting cushioning her body. Opening her journal, she scribbles a title on a blank page in the middle of the book: *Secrets*.

They have returned back home, where she looks around and sees his stationary bike and the dollhouses he made for them, and she smells the wood shavings in the small furnace room adjacent to the stairs.

Alone, she writes, *I miss my daddy Geoffrey Arthur Cragg.*

In the house, she sees him everywhere and nowhere, his presence abruptly removed from their lives. He lingers—his smell, his things, his energy. Like memory, she learns, so too do smells fade away.

He died in a robery, she reports in her journal's newly minted section of things she has learned not to say aloud. *That man who killed him,* she continues, *I hate and I will never forgive him.*

She closes her journal, inserts the key into the lock attached to the book's pastel-pink cover, and walks upstairs.

PLANNING TO TELL
THEM ALL ALONG

I was planning to tell them all along. I really was. In the first meeting with the restorative justice workers, they told me that some people decide never to tell their family, for a number of reasons. Safety. Judgment. The unknown. This was a bit odd; at least, I initially thought so. How could I not tell my family that I was corresponding with the person who murdered our father? It was just a matter of time.

Dinners passed. Gatherings occurred. A year came and went. At the beginning I thought, *I just want to see what this whole thing is about, what it feels like, how I handle it, how we interact.* Once I figured that out, I'd tell them. Later on, I began thinking about how to tell them, but then life happened. Pressing events focused my attention elsewhere.

When it came down to it, there would never have been a good time. So it does not surprise me that I told them because I had to.

My mother, sisters, and I were walking down a familiar winding road to the marine park, waiting for the roast to cook at my mother and stepfather's home while he caught up on work. We regularly went for walks in the dark, dense rainforest along the trails at the opening to Howe Sound.

About a third of the way into our walk as we chatted about nothing special, my mother said, "Girls, I want to tell you something."

Typically, when any of us began a conversation that way, it was something serious, perhaps bad.

"I was talking to a colleague at a work gathering last week. I learned about restorative justice, about this woman who recently died who had contributed significantly to the field. So I got pretty curious and read some of her stuff."

As soon as she said it, I could feel my face begin to heat up and my breathing become shallow. I was walking in front, my sisters in between, and my mother following. I looked forward nervously, not knowing what she was going to say but knowing that my mother was a voracious reader and that when she got an idea in her mind she did a very good job of researching.

"So I called this place, Community Justice Initiatives, spoke with a man named Dave."

Oh God, I thought. *What is she going to say next?*

"So we spoke, and I told him I have this son who's really, really angry at me. And I thought maybe if he did this restorative justice thing, met up with Sheldon, he'd be angry at him instead. He could work through that and be less angry."

That may not be how it works, but okay, Mom, I said to myself.

"Dave said that many prisoners participate willingly in these things. So he told me to ask if your brother wants to participate."

A flood of responses came into my mind. I wanted to say, "I'm pretty sure this is voluntary. You can't just tell a thirty-year-old man to do this, and he'll just go along with it, heal, and all things will be swell. He needs to want to do this."

I wondered what Dave had thought when she'd called him. She and I no longer share a last name, but as soon as she said Sheldon's name, he'd have known she was my mother. *I should write to Dave,* I thought, *and tell him my mother told me she called you.*

"So, girls, what do you think?"

My sisters looked at me. "What do you think?" they said.

"I don't know. What do *you* think?" I looked back at them, but they said nothing. I was trying to practice not stating my opinion first, as they seemed to always rely on me for a response when it came to anything to do with the family. Surely I had begun that dynamic long ago, raising and raging my voice throughout the house as a teenager, continually complaining how awful our family had become. They weren't the least bit interested in my reflections then, no matter what the delivery, but now they looked to me. I had an opinion on everything, and perhaps because of my longstanding history of saying what I thought, they hadn't had a chance to speak. So I was trying to change that. I forced myself to stay silent.

"Do you think he'll want to?" they asked Mom.

"I don't know. I'll see him soon and ask. Carys, what do you think?" she redirected.

I had a decision to make. Was this the situation I had been waiting for? I couldn't *not* tell them now that we'd broached the topic.

"Well," I said, "I know that in restorative justice, people have to want to do this. It's voluntary." I waited and then said as calmly as I could to Mom, "Why would you think of him and not any of us? And what about yourself?"

She considered my question, puzzled. I took note of this alarming fact; she hadn't thought of asking us, not even once. She was focusing on my brother. *How typical,* I thought. And like a small child or a raging teenager, I wanted to yell, "What about me? What about *me?*"

"Sure, perhaps it'll help him. Perhaps it'll hurt him," I said to her instead. "Who knows? Only he can know. It'll be interesting to see what he says."

I was tired of Mom overlooking me—not seeing what I needed. Logically, that would make sense to a desperate mother still in survival mode, wanting to make sure all her children were okay, wanting more of a connection with her angry son. But I wasn't okay, and she'd never known, no matter how loud I screamed it.

"I want to tell you something," I started. I looked at them. "For the past year or so—yeah, maybe a year, since last March—I've been working with Dave. I've been writing back and forth with Sheldon."

I watched for a reaction, turned back, and listened for one. They said nothing. They were not telling me what they were thinking, but surely it was something, I guessed.

"I'll probably meet him sometime soon, but I'm not sure when. I haven't decided yet."

"Oh," my mother said casually, "that's probably why Dave thought Sheldon would be willing to meet your brother."

"Ah, sure. I guess. Whatever." I paused. "So, I've been writing with him, quite a few letters so far. It's been really, uh, interesting, I guess you could say. It's good."

We walked silently a little longer.

"Well," Mom said, "I'd write to him and ask, *Why did you choose our house?* That's all I'd want to ask."

"That's not really where we started. There were quite a few letters back and forth before I asked that, even before we broached the topic of the night itself."

"Are you okay?" one of my sisters asked curiously. It was as though she wanted to take the conversation on a different tangent, but it was already too entrenched.

I felt myself close up. "Yeah, I'm good. Thank you. It's been good."

We continued to walk. I was a bit out of sorts, caught off guard because I had not predicted that this would be the day, the moment I'd tell them what I was doing.

"Remember that woman, Katy?" my mother asked. "Her husband was murdered at that party. In Squamish."

"Yeah, I've actually spoken with her on the phone. I met her at university after one of her presentations about her story. She has an amazing daughter who writes and performs slam poetry. Collects letters from her audiences and sends them to the guy who killed her dad. She was just a toddler when her dad was killed."

I told them what I'd learned from Dave and Sandi, that there are many ways people do this. Some write, some meet. Katy met the guy after five years of silence and secrets in the community. The guy was caught after years of undercover investigations. She was called into the police station after he confessed. He was crying, sobbing when she entered the room, and she said that it took everything in her not to hug him.

We arrived at Whytecliff Park, turned around, and headed back to the house. I trailed close behind the three of them.

"I don't know how much I want to tell you, because I'm in the middle of it all right now. But if you have questions, please ask. I'd be happy to share. I guess I don't know where to start. But for me, I needed to write first."

"If he were doing this," my mother began, still focused on my brother. "If he were doing this—" She paused. "—he could just read your letters and then go meet him."

Her words struck me like a blow to my stomach. Breath left my body and tears filled my eyes. I felt like sinking into the ground.

What was I thinking, I berated myself, wanting her to be curious about me, care about what I was doing? I was stupid for imagining anything had changed.

Immediately I was brought back to my pain in high school. At the school's suggestion, I saw a counsellor, someone who I liked. She taught me that my anger was okay. She saw who I was and what I wanted and told me that was okay.

The counsellor must have been effective, because my mother approached me one day and asked, "Do you mind if I send your sister to her?" My adult self can understand Mom's logic. *One of my daughters is benefitting from this counsellor, so I'll send my other daughter to see her too.* But my adolescent self saw that I was a sacrifice. I wanted so desperately to yell, "There are hundreds of other counsellors in this city. Why can't you find someone else for her? Why do you have to take the good things I do away from me for someone else's benefit?"

A few years after that, back from university, I found myself yelling into the hallway from my bedroom. "What is this? Who did this?"

Five black-and-white landscape shots, inspired by David Hockney's layered approach to photography we'd studied in class, hung askew on my bedroom wall. I'd taken the photographs behind our house, the place I found most calming: the rock face, the moss-covered bluff overlooking the cliff, the arbutus trees, and Howe Sound just beyond. I was proud of these shots, having processed them in the school's photography lab myself and glued them onto thick charcoal-grey matting. But it wasn't the same matting. The corners of the photos curled slightly.

"What is this? Who did this?" I yelled again.

Mom hardly remembered. She said that late one night, desperate about a school project for one of my sisters, they'd needed cardboard matting.

Doing well at school was paramount in my family. This wasn't an explicit rule, no. It was assumed, and our collective perfectionist tendencies reinforced it. Not submitting an assignment on time or in perfect condition was the end of the world. Panic ensued, for it was the only thing we could control. To the outsider, our doing well in school looked good. To us inside, this insidious dynamic had grave effects on our well-being. You could never be good enough. All the effort in the world would never be enough. How do you know when to let go?

In a panic to solve the immediate problem in front of her, my mother had peeled the photos off the original matting and pasted them on flimsy black craft paper. And I learned that perhaps nothing I created was important. Someone else took priority. Nothing was sacred, not even the things I made that connected me to my father.

These memories slowed my steps, and I fell a little farther behind my sisters and mother. They'd never notice, never ask why. Perhaps it was the most hurtful thing she could have said, that she could just take my letters, my words—words I had worked so hard to articulate—and give them to someone else. Then it occurred to me why I had kept my story to myself, sharing it with just a few dear friends. I had been protecting myself from my younger self's pain at being unacknowledged, unseen, having something I was proud of taken away from me.

This is mine, I said to myself. *No one is going to take this away from me.*

I kept walking.

"You're going to go through a series of stages," the counsellor begins. She sits in her seat listening to the woman she recently met with her siblings and mother as a group. Now she sits alone with her in the office, and she's not sure why she has to.

"Eventually," the counsellor continues, "you're going to be very mad at your father for leaving you."

These words fall heavy on her shoulders, a weight she does not wish to bear. She finds the woman both insistent and patronizing, speaking to her as though she has done something wrong. She wants to do what she's supposed to, but it doesn't feel right. She does not know what she has done wrong, but assumes she has; otherwise, why would this person be speaking these words to her?

Please stop talking. I'll deal with my dad's death and his murder in my own way. But she does not yet have the words to say this.

She sits silent, not knowing what to do. She trembles in her seat, wishing her mother would return. When the appointment is over, she tells her mother she does not want to see the counsellor again.

PART FOUR

HEAVE-TO

A maneuver used to slow a sailboat's progress and calm its motion while at sea.

—Blue Water Sailing

FALLING DOWN 15

March 24, 2012

Sheldon,

  I am deeply sad that you did not have a connection with your father,

I began my next letter.

> My dad was a wonderfully talented and flawed man. I look
> forward to how I'll integrate him into my future children's lives
> so they can know him too, in their own way. I want them to
> keep him alive through my stories. I want to teach them what
> he taught me.

I was sad that Sheldon didn't have someone like my dad in his life,
because how else could he know what he took away? Would he have
done what he did if he'd had someone like that in his life? I was sure
that he wouldn't have.

> Did you have that connection with anyone in your life? Someone
> who you look up to, admire, think of with respect?

As I described my dad, I thought back to my efforts to recall his flaws. When my father died, he was idealized into a perfect figure, and I didn't notice the effects of this dynamic until my late adolescence, when I watched my friends with their fathers and felt jealous. They got to be mad at their fathers, argue with them, then hug them and love them the next day.

"What did Dad do wrong?" I asked my mother, trying to understand him as a flawed human being, not an idealized dead one, good at everything. In my twenties, after hearing a handful of stories about his relationship with my mother, I saw how every adventure was my father's, not other people's. I saw how his family's entitlement and privilege—their affluence, his gender, education, class—influenced his choices and the opportunities he had access to. When I asked what he did that wasn't perfect, my mother—even his friends—couldn't, or maybe wouldn't, name a thing. I resented this perfection, how it was impacting me.

"What did you fight about?" And in lieu of any meaningful response, I had to figure out how he and I may have fought. By the absence of fighting, I realized that the chance to have arguments or to be temporarily mad at my father was also taken away from me. I lost a relationship, and I wondered if this man, sitting in prison, had thought about that.

> You know nothing about my dad and the family whose lives you altered forever. Doesn't that seem odd to you? I'm quite mad that this is new information to you. Not mad at you, but mad at the process/system and the structures in place that only allow for this information to be shared after I go through the process of contacting you. All information was cut off way back then, perhaps under the guise of safety for both parties. But with this cutting off of information, something else is lost,

don't you think? Like I said in an earlier letter, I believe part of how you may be able to move forward in life is with knowing who my dad was and continues to be.

You wrote about the morning of September 16, 1992, so I'd like to write of it too. You've told me about that night and the few hours afterward. Let me tell you about what was happening for me those first few hours afterward.

I awoke to screaming. Panicked screaming. My mother yelling, Call 9-1-1. I stayed on the phone as the 9-1-1 responder requested out of concern for my own life and the danger around me. My siblings and mother were with my dad, along with the neighbours who woke up and came outside. They were with him as he bled out, dying on the front lawn. The ambulance and police came. My mother went to the hospital. My siblings and I were taken to the neighbours' house. On the way there, I walked down the stairwell. It was covered in my father's blood. The walls and carpet were covered. This is what I saw. For the next couple of hours I sat shaking in a bathroom, sick to my stomach. I couldn't fall asleep. My mom came back from the hospital in the early morning. She was distraught. She told us that he died. Our life was shattered. I was 11 years old. You inflicted a violent pain upon us. A pain that still hurts today, but in a different, less excruciating way.

I decided to call him out. His reasoning of what occurred that early morning had offended me. I wanted to lay it out, right there for him to see.

I'm sure you've reflected on the existential ridiculousness of how your description sounds from my perspective: That you 'defended' yourself with a weapon in a house that you had no right being in in the first place.

Do you also find it ridiculous that my dad died because you were looking to sustain your livelihood for a few days? Because you needed to get through the next couple of days and you thought it appropriate to carry a knife, my world was ruined. Yours too, but let me just focus on me for a second.

I was a little tired of him focusing on himself, even though I'd been asking him questions about his life. He had never questioned his impact on my family. It had crossed my mind that in none of his letters had he wondered about the logical consequences of his actions. So I told him.

My mother was forced to take care of four kids on a teacher's salary. Friends of my dad slowly disappeared. My brother doesn't have a great male role model to go to for advice, and let me tell you it has had dire consequences that I will not go into. We moved cities, we lost our friends, having to make new ones. We all went into survival mode, in one way or another. No one around me has ever experienced murder—no one gets it. They equate it to a death. Someone died and most people can relate to that. But to be violently traumatized, shaken to your core, no one should have to experience that. Particularly at such a young age. And I'm guessing you know exactly what that feels like, to not live in a peaceful world, to have your safety shaken to your core.

I changed direction to the thing I carried everywhere with me.

My babies will know him but he'll never get to hold them.

This hurt greatly, imagining how much joy I would have brought to my father's life, the pleasure in seeing his smile while he held his grandchild. Tasked to explain how their grandfather died, I imagined myself saying, "A very hurt man hurt your grandfather."

I tell him how my day has gone, but I'll never get to know how his day has gone. He taught me what an education is, but he never got to shake my hand after I graduated from high school, my first degree, or my second degree. He would have really liked that. I don't know how to even begin to describe the depths of pain you've caused me, my family, and the thousands of family, friends, colleagues, patients, and other community members who experienced such a profound loss. I've only scratched the surface, and this is not meant to replace a victim impact statement whatsoever. This is not me yelling at you. This is me informing you of the effects that have occurred in response to your actions.

Did he ever think of that? I wondered.

I guess you couldn't have ever known about the existence of the emotional impact you had on me until I informed you. I think people naturally forget about kids—they're silenced, they're forgotten, they're hidden. But then kids grow up. Your actions devastated our souls, destroyed our confidence, sent us into a spiralling mission to control everything so as to never experience such a life-altering event again, with the implicit expectation that we should bounce back, excel, etc.

More awful than you taking him away from me was you taking me away from him. I made him happy. I made his life better and you took that away from him. In his short 40+ years he did so much. Just think of what he could have done in the future. This is what's on my mind now. If I am blessed to have children one day, he would have been the coolest grandfather. He would have taught them things I could never teach them. But that's enough about that.

I was glad I was saying these things to him, forcing him to reflect on them. They didn't seem to be coming from an angry place, but rather, from an informed, rational place within me.

I find it ironic that the government is willing to spend more on a prisoner's daily life than funding programs. Do you know that as a victim, we had access to something like 500–700 dollars for counselling in response to this event? It's laughable. It's protestable. My family has spent tens of thousands of dollars to keep our well-being intact in response to this event in our lives. No, we as 'victims' are forgotten.

I wish every person's basic needs were met. I clearly have socialist values, and I think rightly so. I wonder what kind of a community we'd live in if every person's basic needs and rights were met. Schooling. Health. Social. We know exactly what people need and we don't give it to them. See who survives and thrives and see who self-destructs and destroys others.

I finished my political rant.

And the ironic thing about it is: This event has become normalized to me. It is now such a significant part of my identity. I understand the world differently than most people I come across. That is incredibly lonely on one level. And as you probably know, it's a useless endeavour to look back and wonder what life would be like if this didn't happen.

This is the information that is kept from you. This is the information that isn't shared in any meaningful way through any of our legal system's structures. The levels of wrong that occurred that night go way beyond you killing my father. The unjust decisions you made that evening go beyond you deciding to use the weapon that had the grave consequence of killing my father. Even you considering coming into my home was an unjust act. The thought itself. Knowing it was a family neighbourhood. Knowing people, children, were in there. Thinking you could just get in and out of there. Breaking in. Walking in. Getting a knife. Walking upstairs. Not running away when you heard noises. Not dropping the knife. Not stabbing him once, twice, three times. You see what I'm getting at. These are all of the acts that lead up to you shattering my family's life.

What is amazing to me is that despite a wrong and unjust act, you had opportunity to make right and just acts. But you continued to do otherwise. Instead of waiting for the police to find you, you could have turned yourself in. Instead of claiming another person killed my dad, you could have not. And instead of lying about your acts for 16+ years, every day you had the chance to tell the truth.

With this momentum, I decided to ask the question that had been quietly gnawing at my mind for years. The question my mother would have asked right out of the gate. I'd put together enough pieces—a phrase from my mother here, a sentence from a counsellor there—to know that no one was offering a straightforward answer.

Over the years I've overheard rumors that you had been a patient of my dad's while he was a resident physician at Foothills, that you may have met him in Emergency there. I also heard that you may have stolen my dad's address at Foothills and that's how you knew to come to my house. Why did you choose our house? University Heights is a family community in Calgary. Lots of kids live in those houses. Who honestly believes you can "get in and out of a house" without disturbing people?

Would he answer it? I did not know. But at least it was out there now. I moved on.

The question you posed—'Was it that I stopped caring about life in general?' I understand that. People give up. They stop caring. Then their actions are of no consequence, and whomever they destroy along the way seems to not be of significance. It seems as though the reason my dad was violently killed was because you needed to get through the next couple of days. Isn't that so awful? So pathetically meaningless. He worked so hard to create a good life for himself and those around him. All of that was taken away—violently—because you needed to get though the next few days.

Writing those words confirmed everything I had done up to that point. Why I had chosen my career. Why I believed what I did. I'd known it when I was younger, after my father died, but I hadn't *really* known it until the offender wrote it in his letter to me. People stopped caring for him, and he fell down. He stopped caring, and my family fell down. The world stops caring, and we all fall down.

What I find fascinating about you is that you continually ask meaningful and thoughtful questions. This is what you did. This is not who you are. This is what happened to me. It is not who I am. But as a result of all of this, here we are, called to do something more meaningful with our lives, by the very existence of both of our circumstances.

Thank you for writing. I will look forward to your response.

Carys

Her mother sends her brother and her to camp for two weeks in the summer before they move back to Vancouver.

There, she is separated from her brother and his friend, boys split apart from the girls. They sleep in groups, in bunk beds in the tipis scattered around the campgrounds. On the first day, the camp leaders ask the girls to pick an activity: hiking, canoeing, or horseback riding. She considers joining the horseback riding group, but there is no room by the time she decides, so she chooses hiking.

They take day and overnight hikes. They sleep on tarps, close to one another, with tarps also hanging over them in an attempt to protect them from the rain. She shivers, trying to warm herself with extra layers of clothing, not able to fall asleep. She listens to the rain patter on the tarp above her and feels the rain soak the corners of the blankets below.

She does not know that while she is at camp, the criminal trial of her father's murderer takes place. Her younger sisters at home have a babysitter. Later, when she asks, her mother tells her that she sent her and her brother to camp so she could focus on the trial, didn't realize that her eldest daughter would have liked to know at the time that the trial was taking place.

Soon after the trial is over, they move back to West Vancouver, where they had lived before moving five years before. She remembers her friends from grade one, but she misses her friends in Calgary, who have also begun their first year at middle school. She does her work, listens to the teachers, and often finds herself staring out the windows. From the side of the mountain where the middle school is perched, she can look out to Burrard Inlet, notice how everything is different, and she must adjust but doesn't know how.

IT'S ABOUT TIME 16

A few weeks later, Jennifer wrote on her fax sheet, *Here is the most recent letter from Sheldon for Carys. Please let us know what comes from your meeting—it would be good to know how she is feeling about things as we move forward.*

I braced myself and began to read.

April 30, 2012

Carys

Well, you seem to have some fully loaded questions on your mind. To answer the first, yes I have had one role model in my life who, I have emulated he was my mother's younger brother, my uncle Mike. He lived with us for such a long time. He was a big guy, he always had a good looking girlfriend and not to mention a nice car. When I was thirteen years old I had noticed he was going in and out of this little blue tool box. When I had gotten the chance to find out what was in there, I went up to his room and opened the door. The box had a number of drugs and paraphernalia of sorts. I proceeded to roll up a joint, stumbled through it to the best of my ability. What I ended up doing was making a terrible mess of the contents of the box. I left the house and went to visit some friends with the big fatty in tow.

I guess I had taken just over a gram and tried to stuff it into a one single little paper. We proceeded to smoke what we could before the high took hold of us. We were all looking at each other like we each had three heads and then I proceeded to laugh because it was the only thing I could do. As the afternoon was a blast and the time went by so quickly, I figured I'd better hit the road. When I walked through the door I was called into the kitchen by my Uncle Mike. I looked up and was surprised to get doused with some hot chicken soup, what a buzz kill. My mother gave him a piece of her mind and then proceeded to yell at me for stealing and smoking drugs. I apologized to my mother but not my uncle. I was very angry with him. If the soup was any hotter I most likely would need a skin graft or two.

He eventually got over the incident but from that day he was always wary of his belongings and precious lock box. I watched him and I learned from him. I found out what he did for a living and wanted to give it a go. So I went to him for advice one day told him I wanted to earn a little extra pocket change. I was about 18 years old at this time. So he told me to meet him downtown. I jumped into his car and we sat there and he told me all there is to know about dealing drugs. At the end of our conversation he pulled out a package. He gave me the pack and told me that he wanted $60.00 a quarter oz. At the time I knew that they were going for $80.00, so I negotiated him down to $40.00. I put the package into my jacket, looked up and saw a 357 magnum staring me in the face. He told me not rip him off and then said I don't care who you are if I mess this up he would shoot me in the face. I reached up and pushed the gun out of my face and told him not to worry. That was the last time I saw him. With the money I made, I moved to Winnipeg, lived there until I moved to Calgary in 1991.

In 1998 I had gotten a phone call from my mother while I was serving time in Prince Albert Penitentiary. She told me they found my Uncle Mike face down in his trailer and someone had ransacked his pockets and stole all his money before they called 911. At the time I took it in stride but then felt this overwhelming sadness. I was able to talk to him over the phone about a month before his death. He spoke to me with a sense of regret and I felt that he truly did miss me and that he did love me. When it finally hit me that I would never see him again I cried for him. Even though his death was because of a heart attack, this was not what made me so emotional, it was the people that went through his pockets as he lay there, maybe with a faint pulse. This was the only man that showed me any kind of understanding. I do miss him but I don't look up to him, not any longer.

I could not comprehend every sentence, yet could entirely comprehend them at the same time. Why couldn't he have had a role model who treated him well so he might have chosen not to treat everyone else like they were worthless, too?

This brings on another topic that you have been grossly misinformed on. I did confess to 2 people about what took place that night. The thought of right and wrong never crossed my mind. I was too busy worrying about my own life. I confessed to someone very close to me that morning after I had gotten home, and I had confessed to a lawyer the day of my arrest.

I wondered, *Who keeps information like that to themselves, only to wreak havoc in a family's life?*

> This justice system didn't care about your family. I wanted to get a manslaughter conviction because I knew that they were going to ask for life. They of course flatly refused. Which made my lawyer pretty angry, and then he came back with a life sentence if I plead guilty. They continue to tell me that it was who I killed, this is what got me the sentence that I had gotten. Let me ask you this if I would of taken some drug dealers life in the same way would they offer me manslaughter. In a heartbeat probably give me a medal for taking another problem off the street.

My dad versus a drug dealer. Was this what he'd just posed to me? Did he want me to feel bad that he'd gotten the sentence he had?

> The penalty I pay for the life I took, hit me the hardest when you came into my life. Let me explain the past statement. I had no prior knowledge of your dad no matter what they tell you. I don't remember your father from the emergency room at the hospital. I wasn't even conscious at the time. I was at the hospital in June of 92 for a car accident. I don't even remember how I got there until 2 days later when I woke up. I didn't steal anything from anybody in order to break into their house 3 months later. If by chance this was your father, then this is truly some coincidental and powerful information. I remember hearing something of this when I went for an assessment to see if I was fit for trial but disregarded it as hostility from the nurses at the hospital I went to.

His words were giving me a familiar rotting feeling in my gut.

> The information you give me pertaining to the relationship
> you had with your father, has become heart wrenching to me.
> But I do believe this is what we have to do in order to come
> to grips with what I did and who I did it to. What I mean is
> without knowing truly who you and your father are and what
> your relationship was I had not thought about it the way I do
> today. Having you tell me how you feel is very important in
> this process no matter how difficult it is for me. It needs to be
> said. You agree?

Yes, I agreed. So wholeheartedly that I wanted to tear through the
letter, across the provinces, and say, "Well, it's about time."

What did he mean, he hadn't thought about it until today? What
if I hadn't introduced myself to him and he'd gone on his way, feeling
unjustly treated because he couldn't get out of the punishment he'd
sought to have dismissed?

Was I helping my father's murderer, helping him process the trauma
he'd inflicted on my father, helping him inch toward wellness with the
true knowledge of what he had done twenty years before?

And then, I thought, was he helping me?

> I can't justify why I did what I did in regards to blaming
> someone else for this crime. I can only tell you that I didn't
> want to be the man that murdered your father and suffer the
> consequences for such a horendouse crime. This is why I have
> agreed to correspond with you this is like therapy for me I know
> that it won't bring your dad back but it will help you express
> those strong emotions that you can't quite describe.

I read the line again: *I didn't want to be the man that murdered your father*. He did all those horrible things because he was so self-involved. He didn't want to be that guy. The guy who killed an amazing man. So he lied about it.

> I have to tell you that I mentioned to a psychologist that I have been corresponding with one of the victims I did not give a name but I felt that I was pressured into disclosing that part. The way things work around here is that psychologists tend to cut and paste a lot of reports. I have a very important hearing coming up and I have to put my best foot forward.

I felt this was a genuine disclosure, something he'd naturally tell his various workers at the prison. I recalled Dave's words to me at the beginning of this journey: "We, Victim Services and the Parole Board of Canada, have a policy in place. Participation in a restorative justice program cannot be used in parole hearings, otherwise the offender could use it to their advantage. The victim needs to be aware of this, so that they can participate fully." I'd believed this, but I was beginning to suspect it wasn't entirely true.

> I told her, if you only know the things that I have done over the years since you last made a report on me. She wanted examples. I felt uneasy but shared them anyway under the guise of her Hippocratic oath. I hope she has some kind of discretionary oath. Once again I sincerely apologise to you for mentioning this to her but writing to you is a huge deal to me. I hope that I will never have to do that again.
>
> The sharing of information is very limited here. I knew absolutely nothing about most aspects of you or your family.

I had a hearing a couple of years ago. This was an attempt to get community service absences to work. I wasn't surprised to see your uncles and mother as I walked into the hearing. What I was told in the hearing is that I could address your family through the parole board. I told them exactly what I did that night. I cried throughout my testimony and told them how very sorry I was. Your mother was in support of my release, which did stagger me just a little. Your uncles, on the other hand, did everything in their power to keep me locked up. I know they hate me for what I did to their brother. This is why I don't blame them for their emotional testimony. One of your uncles went as far as to write a letter to my parole officer here, and tell her just how he felt about my temporary absences. He told her that while he was sitting behind me he could have broke my neck, as he had teachings in some kind of martial arts. He is no longer allowed to come to any more of my hearings as a result. I feel sad for that because he no longer has an outlet to express to me how he feels.

I know that you have nothing to do with your uncles but I wanted to let you know how information flows to me. Unless something significant happens I hear nothing about you or any other members of your family. My only outlet is what you tell me. I have only heard that you and your family moved to BC a long time ago. I can't say who told me this because I don't even remember.

Did you know that the average family makes $75,000 a year and has to give 40% of that income to 1 form or another of government. What kinds of expenses are you people paying for out there. I can't imagine giving 40% of my income to the government, so that they can jet set all over the world on my hard earned money. Sorry I got off topic I read this in the paper today. I have it made here and I get free food and a roof over my head. I don't have to pay for electricity. I work my fingers to the bone almost every day; I haven't seen my family in over two years. I have to do what I'm told even if I find it degrading and in humane. I can't have an opinion or I will find myself locked up in a cell for days on end. Although I haven't used drugs in over 6 years I am always suspected and have to give urinanalysis test every month.

I have all kind of health issues, because I lack motivation. Not to mention the social consequences I have to endure when I work in the community. They make it so degrading for a person. The supervisors you work for are hesitant to hire you. I can't phone my family to talk to them when I need to express myself. There are only 2 phones for 70 inmates here and they are only on certain times of the day. I sometimes don't even feel emotions for things that I should. I will see something on T.V. like a child losing her life because some man took it upon himself to abuse and murder her. The next thing I know this man has been bludgeoned to death in the cell down the hall. But I feel nothing for him Why should I he killed an innocent girl. Is this how your uncles think of me? I don't want to be that person, do you have any advice on this topic that may help me cope with your reality. I have no problem coping with mine.

Thank for listening.

Sheldon

W e're going to move on from limericks today," the English teacher instructs her class of grade seven students. "Does anyone know what a haiku is?" The class remains silent. "Well, this is my favourite type of poetry. These poems hold such wonderful meaning in their short passages."

She watches her teacher.

"This is how these poems work. There are seventeen syllables, split into three lines." She illustrates the structure of the haiku, writing on the board. "Does anyone have any questions?"

"Do you mean five words, seven words, five words?" a girl with a confused expression asks.

"No, not quite. Five syllables, seven syllables, five syllables," the teacher corrects and reviews the sounds of words. She gives a few examples to further explain the concept. "Okay, now that we've gone over the basics, I want you to try to write one. You'll have about twenty minutes."

Five minutes, ten minutes, fifteen minutes pass.

I don't know what to write, she thinks. She overhears the boy next to her whispering to his neighbour.

She refocuses on the blank page in front of her. Her heart beats faster. She notices herself taking fewer breaths.

"Okay, you have two more minutes, everyone, and then I'd like you to hand them in," the teacher calls out.

A wave of calm rushes through her. *Daddy.* She positions her pencil, tunes out the chattering voices surrounding her, and writes.

> We all had good times.
> He was loving and was loved.
> But he had to go.

Her eyes widen as she reads it over. *It needs a title,* she decides.

As the teacher calls out, "Okay, everyone, hand them forward," she quickly scribbles on the top of the page, "Lost."

THE RIGHT TIME

I'm ready to send you out now," Dave had said to me confidently only a couple of letters into our correspondence. While I thought that was supportive and indicated a confidence in the process, I knew that I wasn't ready. I would know when. So I waited, for some time.

After five letters sent and five letters received, four hundred and eighty-two days since first asking Dave to begin this process, I finally felt the offender and I had entered a space where something had emerged that had not existed at the outset.

"I'd like to meet him," I said, confidently. "I think it's the right time."

"You bet," Dave said.

"I've been thinking about a day. It will be an important day, one I will remember. I've decided that it should be September 17, the day after the date my dad died."

"Great, we'll make that happen," said Susan. Like Sandi, who had recently retired, Susan had a kind presence and a calm demeanour, waiting for cues during our conversations to delicately jump in.

"But I don't want you to say this to him—the part about the date. I want to ask him in the letter."

"We can do that. Jennifer will take the letter and give it to him, and after he reads it she'll inquire about booking that day. We'll take care of the details."

"What do you need from me?"

"Just send us a copy of your identification. We'll get you to fill out a visitor's form. They'll have to clear you, do something like a criminal records check."

"That's it?" I smiled. "Do you think that day will work out? On the administrative side of things?"

"I don't see any problem with it. There's enough time."

I returned home and wrote the letter.

July 15, 2012

Sheldon,

What's really odd for me is that before I began to write to you, I really didn't have much to say. I never thought of what I may say, never planned what I may ask you, but as soon as I began to write, as soon as I allowed myself to do this, there were all of these things I wanted to say and ask.

In your last letter, you mentioned telling the psychologist about this process. As long as you act with honesty and good faith, I feel fine about that. You have every right to represent this process in whatever way you wish and to whomever you want.

I guess that I just don't want to be hurt by any of this—some people I've told have been more supportive and encouraging than others and I can't tell you how much it hurts when people don't support what I'm doing. Since last writing to you, I've told most of my most immediate family about this process—they're not against what I'm doing. But my family is not encouraging me nor curious. They're different than I am when it comes to what I want to learn about the world. Perhaps they'll ask to see these letters in 10 years. My friends are much more supportive, which is very grounding and makes me feel like some people understand what I'm seeking. And it makes me feel very happy to know that the friends in my life right now completely understand what I'm all about.

Perhaps I should address some of the things you mentioned in your last letter, as they were quite powerful. You've made me think a lot about the anger some of my extended family feels towards you. Previous to this, just thinking about the anger they embody made me feel really sick. I worry about the lives they've hurt, how horrible their relationships are, how much destruction they've caused for themselves and others, way before you ever came along, and it's just continued. I had a lot of anger in me when I was younger—not directed at you, ironically. Home, to say the least, was cold and unresponsive, and for that I was very, very angry. Little did I know that they were just not able to respond to what I needed—this is what I'm learning now. Anyway, about the anger, maybe you can understand their experience of anger. And maybe, along with hearing from me, you have to hear from them, and combined you'll make sense of that experience.

I do agree with you that no matter how difficult hearing the information I share about the relationship I had/have with my father, it's necessary and important for you to hear. I feel like I'm honouring my dad's life by doing this, which is necessary for my life to move forward.

You mentioned the issue of who you killed—a contributing family physician—and as though the justice system—its police, lawyers, Acts—values some people more than others. You're right. For geographic and political reasons (Alberta conservatism) and social reasons (physician vs. drug dealer), you have a very long sentence. What I hate about that is implicitly our society values people differently. I'm obviously biased—you took away someone who made my life amazingly rewarding; but the drug dealer you speak of has a daughter who looks up to him, who would be traumatically devastated if you took him away from her, and she'd probably have some pretty strong opinions about that and about rehabilitation. What I won't concede is that a drug dealer—a person—is valued less by way of a lesser sentence. As far as I'm concerned, both lives are worth everything, and if I believed a long-term prison sentence actually rehabilitated people, I'd say that both lives deserved 25-year sentences.

What would make me feel better about this is if I knew for sure you don't embody anger. I mean, we all get angry. It's a very useful human emotion, particularly in response to injustice. But the seething, blowing up at everything and everyone kind of angry is scary, dominant, and can only lead to further destruction. This destruction makes me so unbelievably scared. What scares me even more is when people stop caring about their lives and others. To know that someone else's anger could ruin my life at any given moment freaks the hell out of me.

I'm glad you have access to the newspaper information you mentioned. I think it's a privilege to give personal income to the community, to support necessary care that we all need to live together. I just don't like it when it's spent poorly—say, on extended incarceration, despite all scientific evidence saying that intervention doesn't rehabilitate. Or when it's not spent on things I feel are necessary—say, on family support and development, so children don't grow up in survival mode, only to repeat what was given to them.

With that said, I feel that because of the conversation we've had over a significant amount of time, I'm ready to ask you if it would be okay if we could meet. I think there's been enough emotional safety in the pace of the conversation for us to now meet. Days are very important to me. While I'm not a religious person, I've always respected various religions and spiritual traditions for creating meaning out of days. Death anniversaries are very important to me. Like my dad's death day. I now treat this day very much like new year. Because honestly, my life as I knew it ended on that day and began anew on the next. I am willing to guess that yours did too.

Because of this, I'd like to propose that we meet this coming Monday, September 17th. If the day before, for me, means to honour death, then perhaps we could make the day after a way to honour life.

To be honest, I am not afraid of meeting you, but I am apprehensive anticipating how I'll feel. There are some things that I'd like to ask you that don't really work, at least for me, in a letter.

I'd like to ask you to describe the night before you came into our house, what you were doing around that area, why you chose us, the event itself, what you did after, and perhaps your experience of the aftermath, including the trial. I'd also like to ask you about your current experience of prison. You've mentioned things and I'm curious to know more about them—helpful programs, helpful people, things you're working towards.

In one of your first letters you mentioned that you wouldn't be able to look me in the eye. I hope you can.

Thank you for writing.

Carys

Sitting in her bed, she props her back up against the wall with a pillow. Tears run down her face. She cannot believe what's happened, again.

The night before, she returns from the hospital where her older cousin was taken by ambulance after his fatal cliff jump at Whytecliff Park into the waters of Howe Sound, the same cliff where she and her friends jumped just weeks before. She can still feel his cooling skin when she brought her face up to his, while he lay on the emergency room gurney, and whispered in his ear, "I'll never say goodbye."

The house is empty; her mother and siblings are out. She knows now that she must deal with this loss on her own. Reaching over to her desk, she grabs some paper and a pen, leans back against the wall, and writes to her father.

> Daddy,
> He died yesterday. I don't know if he is with you yet, but he will be. Tell him I say hi. And that I love him. And please tell the person who controls all of this (if there is one) to screw himself. Daddy, I am so confused. I don't understand why. He was so beautiful. So smart, so kind, and everything else. What do I do? What should I learn from this? How is everyone going to deal with this? He shouldn't be gone. It wasn't his time. And you too. Oh my god. This is so much. I just keep crying and crying. I know I can get through this, but I don't get why I have to. Why does everyone keep leaving me? It hurts too much. I am so afraid. I mean who is 'he' going to take next? Please talk to him and tell him to stop it. I haven't done anything wrong.

Ever. Daddy, what should I do? I'm so sorry for not writing longer. It's just I can't stop crying. I love you so much, and tell that to him.

Love,

Carys

She folds the paper up, and on top of it she writes, *I've Had Enough*. She lays her head down on the pillow, brings her knees close to her chest, and wraps her arms around them. She closes her eyes and tries to fall asleep.

At his memorial service, she sings for her cousin, for her father, for all the lost ones she misses and carries around with her everywhere she goes.

18
BEST INTENTIONS

A week later Sheldon responded, and I travelled to Langley to read it.

July 22, 2012

Carys,

Hello, I would like to start off by telling you that I have no apprehensions about us meeting. I have known that this would happen eventually. The part I am kind of concerned about is your pre-conceived notion of what I may look like. If there was a boogie man, you probably think that he looks pretty intimidating. He may be a big man, with darkness surrounding him. He's probably carrying a huge blade in his hand. I don't know what you expect to see, but the last thing I want to do is scare you upon meeting. So, I would like to tell you that I do have an intimidating presence at first glance. This is due to the masks I have been wearing while living in this environment. What I can tell you is I have only the best intention when it comes to meeting you and I don't want you to have any discomfiture.

While writing to him, I'd never considered his appearance, because years before I had searched the internet for information on him and found a group photo of many large men, like a school photo. It looked as though the prison had partnered with a local trade program and an industry sponsor, and nine or so prisoners had graduated. Many looked like they'd been lifting weights for some time, with their barrel chests and thick torsos. Diplomas hung from their hands, and I recall seeing closed-mouth smiles, squinting eyes. They looked strong and serious, as though if someone said something wrong all hell would break loose. The men flanking them were dressed in suits and button-up shirts. It was clear who were the prisoners and who were the supervisors.

Beneath the photo was a series of names, including Sheldon Klatt. His body was large, overweight, and his face not entirely distinguishable. I'd read somewhere that prisoners often gain weight for protection from others, protection from self. Strangely enough, he looked like the friendliest of the group.

I like the idea of incorporating topics for which to discuss upon your arrival. I would like to hear all about what you do. I do have one topic that you deserve to be aware of. As you know with the life sentence that was thrust upon me, also gave me an opportunity to apply for a faint hope clause review. In 2007, I had an application for this review submitted to the powers that be. This application has gone through the courts and now has come full circle. I will be going back to court to see if I can get my parole eligibility date sooner than 2017. This court case will surely involve the media, your family and a plethora of buried memories and emotions for you.

Maybe he was trying to communicate that he was trying to imagine my experience. But I recoiled at the psychobabble: *buried memories and emotions.* I wondered if he'd learned this language from prison therapy. I knew enough from my own training to recognize the words he integrated into the information he shared. I wanted to say, "Well, clearly they're not buried. I'm speaking to you about them, rather articulately."

> This is not a fly by the night hi and bye court case. This will be a lengthy process. I have to explain what I've done to be granted such a privilege. This is done in front of a jury, a judge and anybody else that has taken an interest in my case. As I have said, I had applied for this in 2007. Since 2007, a lot has changed for me. I have been estranged from my family and my plans to live there have fallen at the wayside. I have told my parole officer what has happened and I will be discussing this with her in depth very soon. I have basically washed my hands with them. They blame me for everything, and when I say everything, I mean everything that happens in their lives.

Strange, I thought, they sounded like my father's family.

> I have been their whipping post for way too long. I need to show myself that I can make it out there. Then they will realize that I have changed. They think that where ever I decide to live I could never be accepted. I can't get credit from a bank to get a loan. I told them I don't need a loan, and that I plan on going back to school. They tell me that no school will ever take me after they find out where I've been. I told them that this was an inaccurate statement.
>
> Now on a brighter topic, you had mentioned something about anger. You are right. Anger can be a disruptive emotion.

The aggression is an act of that emotion. I will not act on my emotions, there are times when frustration rears its ugly head and my speech becomes louder, but I will never raise a hand to express my anger. If there is a debate in progress and I need facts to prove my case, then I will surely seek out those facts and bring them to the forefront.

Sept 17 will be just fine. The only thing I have to do is make sure that my lawyer does not book that day for any kind of court proceeding. I have basically opened my life to you, and as you may not know I am a very reserved person when it comes to opening up to people. So I think that looking you in the eyes is the least of my worries. So I will be seeing you then literally speaking.

Thanks for writing,

Sheldon

PS I have enclosed a photo of myself so you will know what I look like.

"There's a photo?" I said to Dave and Susan.

"Yes. We have it in this file if you'd like it," Dave said.

"No, I don't want a photo of him," I said without a second thought. "What is he talking about, *court proceedings*?"

"We don't really know, probably to do with applying to the Parole Board for more escorted releases."

"He makes it sound like he's getting out of prison soon," I said. I knew this wasn't true. As a registered victim, I was informed of all leaves, Parole Board reviews, and applications months in advance of any hearing. But the uncertainty unsettled me nonetheless.

I thought about it for a few more minutes as Dave and Susan, patient as always, waited for me to process Sheldon's words. *Why was I stuck on this?* Laughing at myself for wanting to be in control, to have access to all information that may affect me, I rolled my eyes and spoke under my breath as I got up to leave the office.

"Maybe he's just hopeful."

She sinks slowly down onto the surface of the kitchen floor. The sun has set, and the dark glow of the horizon closes in on the room. Her family is out: her brother is at work, and her mother is driving her sisters to gymnastics lessons. She is left alone in the cold, empty, quiet home. She doesn't know, or care, where her friends are that Saturday night.

She squishes her face, attempting to expel the tears suspended in her eyes. She grabs at the hardwood floor, wishing it would give—just a little—to take the pain out of her body. To anywhere else.

She lies there, face down, knees tucked into her chest, pushing down.

Outside darkens. *How long have I been lying here?* she thinks to herself.

Pushing her palms against the floor, she lifts herself up, drags the hair off her face, ripping it away from the dried tears. Standing, she rests her hands on her hips, as if to hold herself up. She feels empty.

Stretching her shoulders back, raising her chin up, she looks around. She walks to her bedroom and sits at her desk. She opens her notebook, looks down at the blank page in front of her, and begins to write.

> In case I don't remember in 30 years. I just cried for like an hour on the kitchen floor.

She puts her notebook back into the desk drawer, slides underneath the covers of her bed, and closes her eyes.

PART FIVE

TAKEN ABACK

Where the wind is blowing into the sails 'backwards,' causing a sudden (and possibly dangerous) shift in the position of the sails.

—Sailing Terms, NauticEd

SEPTEMBER 16, 2012

I returned home and thought about the photograph. There was no way I wished to hold a photograph of him, nor did I wish to keep it in my home. That seemed beyond inappropriate, like bringing work documents I wasn't supposed to take out of the office. *No, Dave can keep that*, I thought.

Kneeling in front of my living room console where I kept family photographs, I slid the cupboard door to the side and shuffled through the piles. Family DVDs were stacked atop one another, converted from VHS tapes my father recorded, lugging a massive video camera on his shoulder. His kind voice asking us questions, curious about what we were doing as as he followed us around the house, was captured forever. Next to the videos were boxes and files, and in the files I kept a few special pictures of my family.

I flipped through them and stopped at my favourite photograph of Dad. He wears blue jeans and a worn long-sleeved brown shirt. He sits leaning against the wall next to the entrance of a cabin, his feet relaxed on the steps below. He is fixing my mother's broken necklace. He smiles a big grin, just like he always did. Just like I always do.

I looked once more at the photograph, then at one of my father holding my sister upside down in the backyard, massive grins on their faces. Our family Christmas card, with of all of us in a big pile of raked leaves.

Another of our sun-kissed faces, with Howe Sound in the background, the land where he had planned to build us a house. I stared deeply into each photo and recalled each moment as tears blurred my vision. All I saw was his smile.

I whispered to myself, "He took away all the joy."

"Carys, for this year's anniversary, I think we should invite just a few special people—our old friends, Dad's friends—to Larson Bay." We'd gathered there one year after his death to celebrate his life, where his friends dedicated two benches, a drinking fountain, and a rock with a plaque to him. "What do you think?" Mom asked me over the phone.

"I think that's a great idea," I said.

"Should we gather in the evening? It'll be a beautiful day."

Five years before, when my father's old friend—with whom he'd sailed from Auckland to Vancouver—took us out to Larson Bay on Dad's death anniversary, it had been a beautiful day. We'd anchored in the bay, had lunch, and then passed the bag with my father's ashes through each of our hands before pouring them into the sea. He'd asked to be scattered in the ocean.

I wondered if Mom remembered what I'd told her a month earlier. "Could we have it in the daytime? I'm flying to Calgary that evening. I'm going to the prison the following day," I reminded her.

"Oh, right. Yes, of course we can do that," she said.

"Thank you."

On the day of the twentieth anniversary of his death, my mother and I stood arranging lunch food on picnic tables, trying to make the place look presentable—some combination of beautiful and reflective.

My siblings had gone to get more food and blankets while Mom and I awaited our guests. The sun shone, the water lapped, and the air was brisk. We glanced north to the tall trees hiding wooded trails, and then south to the Salish Sea.

This public beach was never busy, perhaps because all signage to it was continually removed by the locals. Two women appeared, walking up the gravel terrain. They looked our way, saw the tables, flowers, food, and us.

"What are you celebrating?" one of them asked.

My mother looked at me. I replied, "My dad's death anniversary."

"Oh," she said with what seemed like sympathy. "How did he die?"

I knew they expected a *pretty* response, something politiely veiled that they could leave behind as they continued their walk up the hill, enjoying the beautiful outdoors.

"He was murdered." Perhaps this sentence came from an ugly place, from wanting to put them in their place for entering the private space we'd created. But then I thought, *No, they asked, and I told them the truth. I should be comfortable saying it, and they should learn to be comfortable hearing it.* I would not be polite. *It is how he died,* I thought.

"Oh," they both said timidly, shifting to the side—not rushing away but not continuing the conversation either.

Murder seemed to be a conversation stopper, I had noticed over the past twenty years. Surely if I was visibly comfortable sharing that he was murdered, then they shouldn't retreat into their own fear, veiling it in so-called concern that asking further questions would hurt us. Such responses seemed more about their discomfort than about connecting with us. I wished they would just place their hands on their hearts, hum as they let out their breath, look us in the eye and say, "Ah, then you're survivors," and be on their way.

As they walked up the hill, I looked at my mother. We acknowledged each other's implicit understanding that some people just don't know how to handle the topic and seem not to want to learn. It's a strange camaraderie created between people who have lived through trauma. I hated that I judged those women for being afraid, for not knowing what to do. Murder was like any other topic to us, but clearly that was not the case for everyone.

"Carys, once everyone has gathered and eaten a bit and caught up, what should I say to toast Geoff?"

I thought for a few moments, and then it came to me. "You know that story you told me from Dad's celebration of life in Vancouver twenty years ago?"

I didn't remember the speeches my father's friends gave. Had I sat and listened to what people said? Or did the adults forget to gather the children from the lawn of the yacht club, where they were running around? No one can tell me, for they, too, don't remember.

"How Dad's friend told everyone about his drive to the service," I continued. "Seeing that guy running or biking along the way. How does it go?"

"Oh yes, that was one of your dad's best friends. I'll get some details wrong, I'm sure."

"That's okay," I said. *People will like to be reminded,* I thought.

She began, "He was driving to the service, and he saw a guy minding his own business, biking along the road in the same direction. He thought to himself, *This guy isn't feeling what I'm feeling. This guy hasn't just lost an incredible man in such a horrible way.* He thought, *I'm so jealous of this guy who doesn't have to feel what I'm feeling right now. Feeling all of this pain that we're all feeling.* He kept driving. And then he realized that the guy didn't know Geoff. He didn't get to be his friend. He didn't get to know him and be loved by him. And eventually he realized, *I feel sorry for this guy, because he didn't get to have Geoff in his life.*"

I held my chest. "Yes, that's exactly what you should say."

Everyone is out at their weekend activities, and she is at home. She enters her mother's bedroom closet and sits on the floor, takes the boxes off the small wooden chest, and brushes dust off the lid.

Her mother calls the boxes hope chests. She has asked for one from her mother for Christmas. She likes the idea of keeping her collections in a wooden box to look at later, and for her future children to look at after she dies: photos, trinkets, and keepsakes—items of no particular meaning to anyone but her.

She lifts the rustic lock up and pushes the lid back, leaning it against the wall. The hinge creaks. The smell of her father envelops the space. She scans the contents: rosin for his violin bow, assorted fine hand-held tools, a stethoscope, many photographs, small plastic boxes full of negatives, and incomplete, illegible, pocket-sized journals. Gently removing some of the photos, she holds them atop her palms. Thick card stock brushes together, the ends of the photos curved from age. She knows her father developed them himself many years ago.

She looks at the photo on top of the pile, the one she placed there months ago, when she last accessed the chest. He stands tall in his worn jeans, his dark brown hair shaggy, holding a camera to his eye. Is he at the aquarium in Stanley Park? Who is taking the photo of him? He is in his mid-twenties, maybe. She begins flipping through the photos. She laughs at the silly photo-booth strips, at his moustache and shaggy 1970s haircut. She continues flipping. She recognizes the background of an eight-by-eleven photograph. It is Jericho Beach, where her father was a lifeguard when he was young. He was always near the water. He grips the pipe of the outdoor shower like a gymnast on the horizontal bars midway through a pullover flip. His teenage body is lean and strong. His face is young.

She smiles, likes knowing about the things he did.

NO ONE 20 ELSE BUT ME

Dave and I waited just outside the baggage claim area at the Calgary airport for Jennifer. When she arrived, I hugged her instinctively. "Jennifer, it's so nice to finally meet you," I said. She had read every thought that had passed from my mind to his, had carefully escorted my letters to him and brought his back to me, had written kind notes on the fax cover pages.

We decided to get dinner at the airport, as Drumheller was unlikely to have anything open at that hour. As we sat down in a nearby restaurant that was open to the atrium in the airport, a number of passengers were scurrying by. I wondered where they were all going. I wondered if they, too, were going to visit their father's murderer.

"I thought I'd go over a few details of how tomorrow will look," Jennifer said.

"Yes, that'd be great." I had no idea what to expect. I hadn't prepared a thing. I somehow thought that I would know what I needed to say. It was the first time in years that I hadn't written out a list of questions ahead of time.

"We'll be in a boardroom in the administrative building," she began. The setting apparently did not look like a prison. She tried to explain the exterior, how there were many one-storey buildings where groups of men lived. She told me that we likely couldn't bring food with us and that we'd have to go out for lunch.

"Where are the washrooms?" I asked, not knowing where the question had come from but knowing that if I knew some of the basics, I'd feel more comfortable, safer.

"Right across the hall. I'll show you when we get there." She continued to review details. "There's a probation officer whom Sheldon has known since he was young. She has an office right next door to the boardroom. You'll also see a family meeting room with a television, kids' chairs, and a phone." She also said I should keep personal items in the car, and anything I wanted to take in I should give to her, as the guards were more likely to approve what she was carrying. "No phones, though."

I had assumed as much.

"I told Sheldon we'd want to begin around nine, so we'll have to leave the hotel at eight or so."

"Do you mind if we stop for a coffee?" I asked. I realized that I wanted my morning routine to be the same.

"Sure. Let's be ready by seven-thirty, and then we'll go find something." That meant I would need to wake up by six-thirty. I was not a morning person, never had been, so this would be a challenge.

It was dark by the time we left the airport and headed north out of the city, beginning the hour-and-a-half-long drive. Dave seemed to doze off in the back seat, leaving Jennifer and me alone to talk. We took the exit off the main highway heading east, the single-lane road that would take us straight to Drumheller. All I could see was what the headlights illuminated: glimpses of farmland, water towers, and bales of hay scattered along the land.

"In one of your letters, you mentioned shaking his hand when you meet him," Jennifer said.

"Oh, right. I've been thinking about that. Maybe I'll decide to shake his hand later, but I don't want to touch him at the beginning. I think that may overwhelm me in some way I can't predict."

"No problem. I'll let him know."

"How does the conversation start? Do people feel nervous? What if there's nothing to say? So much was said in the letters."

"You'll know what to say. We know you, and you'll know what to do." Her and Dave's confidence in me meant everything. "Do you have any other questions?"

"I really don't know. How do you know what to ask, when it's something you've never done before?"

"Oh, I understand completely. How about I just keep covering different things?"

"Yes," I said. "That'd be really helpful."

At the motel, we went to our separate rooms. I realized the next time I saw them, we'd be on our way to the prison.

I put on my pyjamas and then looked through my file folder full of letters. I wanted to reread all of them, as only the last few letters were fresh in my mind. It was around eleven o'clock when I started, and I didn't anticipate how long it would take to get through all of them. *Maybe I should have done this on the plane,* I thought.

As I read, I was reminded of details, questions, and the sheer volume of words we'd shared with each other over a year and a half of writing. After I finished, I climbed into bed and soon after closing my eyes, I crashed.

I went through my regular morning routine of showering, blow-drying my hair, and applying makeup. Dressed in a striped grey and yellow knee-length pencil skirt, charcoal sweater, and my favourite lightweight fall jacket, I looked at myself in front of the mirror and ran my fingers through my hair. I'd finally found a haircut that suited the shape of my face.

Is it strange to want to look good when meeting your father's murderer? I laughed at this idea. *But I like these clothes,* I argued with myself. I liked the retro cut of the jacket and its two oversized buttons—one missing, but I wore it anyway. *I wear these things to feel like myself,* I thought. *I look good for no one else but me.*

It took seven minutes to drive from downtown Drumheller along the highway and turn left onto Institution Road. We pulled over to wait because we were early.

"Can they see us from here?" I asked.

"No, we're still a fair distance away," Jennifer said, pointing to the buildings in the distance, the equivalent of a few city blocks away.

We sat in silence in the bright morning light. Behind us, farmland stretched all the way to the city. To our left, I scanned the alternating layers of eroding sand, mudstone, coal, and shale that seemed to go on forever into the distance. In front of us stood the grounds that housed two prisons, medium- and minimum-security. And to our right, the foothills rolled far into the distance, where nothing obstructed our view; I imagined that just beyond were the Rocky Mountains that stood between the province of Alberta, where my old life ended in an instant, and British Columbia, where my new life began.

"Well, should we go?" Jennifer asked.

"Yes," I replied.

We drove slowly along the road and passed the main security check. I saw small, one-storey portable buildings to my left and a larger prison block just beyond, as Jennifer had said there would be.

"That's the medium-security prison," she said. "How about I go around behind there so you can see it?"

We drove slowly as though we were on a sightseeing tour, and I noticed the tall fences with coiled razor wire on top. I appreciated the slow approach onto the grounds. I had been told that this was where he'd lived for some time, before being transferred up the road to the minimum-security units.

We passed what looked like the administration building that Jennifer had described the night before. A large greenhouse was nearby, as well as what looked like a garage, an open shelter that housed building materials, tractors, and machines.

Eight or so small portable homes sat behind the administrative building, parallel to the highway. There were no fences to stop the prisoners from leaving. Yet, I was told, they didn't leave. They needed to learn to live together. In these home-like structures, they shared kitchens and living rooms, ate meals together. They returned home after their escorted temporary absences for work.

We pulled up slowly into the gravel parking lot. I could feel the tiny rocks spewing out from underneath the tires. As we placed our personal items in the trunk, I became increasingly mindful that he could see we'd arrived. I looked around.

"Can he see us?" I asked Jennifer.

"No, he'll be inside. He can't come out until I call for him."

We walked alongside the waist-high gates of the white-painted wire fences and passed by the picnic tables and child-sized patio chairs meant for family visits. Inside the building, Jennifer checked in with the guards, and then we walked straight to the boardroom. I peeked into the adjacent room. A woman with short dark hair stood at her desk. We looked at each other for a split second. I closed my eyes and lowered my head.

"That's his parole officer, like I mentioned," Jennifer said, as we sat down in the boardroom. "She'll be there the entire time." She paused. "You tell us when you're ready."

I thought back to the previous day's gathering, in that beautiful bay on British Columbia's coast. My mother had let slip to an old friend of hers and of my father's: "Carys, tell her what you're going to go do tomorrow."

As soon as she said it, she knew she'd done something wrong. Perhaps it was the look I gave her. I had perfected this harsh stare over the years, a thousand words rolled up into a single expression.

"I want you to know that I feel comfortable talking with people about what I'm doing," I said to my mother. "I will tell her what I'm doing before the other guests arrive, but today is about Dad. It's about celebrating his life and the meaning it has in our lives. Tomorrow is about what I've been doing, but today is about Dad." I paused.

"Okay," my mother responded, clearly aware of the stern direction she had just received from her opinionated, headstrong daughter.

I then turned my attention to the friend. "Tomorrow, after a year and a half of writing letters back and forth, I'm going to visit Dad's murderer at Drumheller Institution," I said with a strange calm.

The friend was silent for a moment, and then asked, "What are you expecting from doing this?"

I'd heard this question before. The question, to me, implied something fully loaded. They imagined that I was hurt, that I wanted retribution, that I expected an impossible healing and would be sorely disappointed.

I took a deep breath. "To be honest, I don't expect anything. Nothing. I just need to do this." She didn't say anything in return, but simply nodded. My mother nodded too. They seemed to get it.

Afterward, my mother told me that she and her friend were satisfied with my response, thought it mature of me. This, of course, made me mad: Why should it be up to them to be satisfied with what I was doing? It was condescending, as though I needed everyone's explicit permission to do this. The experience reminded me of the apprehensive responses from others I'd told, and the implicit looks asking, "Are you a masochist?"

"It'll be overwhelming," some said, on more than one occasion.

"It'll be painful," said others.

It seemed as though the idea of experiencing anything intense was permissible if it happened *to* you but not if you invited the possibility into your own life. That was just crazy. *They are just being protective,* I reassured myself and dismissed them from my mind.

I looked down at my hands resting in my lap. I smiled, which caused tears welling in my eyes to fall out and then run down my face. As I dried them with the back of my hand, I announced, "I'm ready."

She flips through the videotapes in their basement playroom, reading her mother's handwriting: *Kids '84, Christmas '86, Transpac '86.* She stops, noting that she has not seen this one before. She inserts the tape into the VHS player.

She hears sails flapping and gusts of wind. Open waters surround a sailboat that she does not recognize as it travels in the Transpacific Yacht Race from Long Beach, California, to Honolulu, Hawaii.

She remembers sitting in *Tangerine*'s cabin, leaning back, holding the seat below her as the boat pitched up and down. She remembers the tingling in her neck, a mild nausea rising from her belly to throat. Waves crash against the hull. Rain slams against the cabin's wooden door.

"Come up here, guys! You'll feel better," her father shouts from above. He holds the wheel, standing in the cockpit, and they emerge from the companionway.

While the storm scares her, her stomach immediately feels relief. They are somewhere between the mainland and Texada Island, in the middle of the Salish Sea. She likes seeing the waves crash against the boat, likes feeling the rain and wind hit her face. Her eyes widen.

She grips the shoulder straps of her thick life jacket and sits on the cockpit's bench. She listens to the ropes tightening, the winches ratcheting, the sails stretching, and the rigging rattling in the wind.

Her dad yells, "Whoo-hoo!"

WHAT MY DAD WOULD DO

"Offender Klatt," the guard said over the intercom. Alone in the room, I stayed silent as I heard mumbled voices making what sounded like introductions. A few moments later, Jennifer knocked as she opened the door and returned to her seat. Pressure rose in my chest. Soon after, Dave knocked too, peeked his head in, and asked if they could enter. Even though I had the option to say no, I said yes.

Dave entered and Sheldon followed.

He had closely shorn light brown hair and was plainly dressed in blue jeans, a white T-shirt, and a navy blue track suit jacket with a white stripe that ran from the collar to his wrists. He seemed short, with a stocky, thick build, and a light-skinned, square face, cleanly shaven. He looked young and seemed nervous.

"Hi," he said as he leaned over the wide table, extending his hand.

I shifted my gaze to Jennifer. and she quickly noticed. "No touching, I forgot to say."

"I'm as nervous as hell," he said. His voice was quiet, light. He lifted his hands and placed them on the top of Dave's designated chair.

Dave pulled out the other chair, gesturing for him to sit there.

"As I said to both of you, just take a minute to get used to being in the same room together," Jennifer said

Dave jumped in. "You know, it's normally a process that works for both parties. We're here for the both of you. What can be done to bring about some healing from the pain in the past? There's something about having shared so much in the letters but not having yet met. I'm wondering if either of you wants to start or say what you're hoping to get out of today."

I thought about the question, then addressed Sheldon. "I'm just hoping to meet you, and if that's what I get out of today, then that's already been accomplished. So whatever the rest of the day looks like, I'm going to be asking some questions. I know Dave uses the term 'healing,' and I don't know if I'm entirely sold on that, but I'm interested in spending some time here and seeing you as a person."

"That's not why I'm here either," Sheldon said. "I've lived with it for years and years, wanting to bang my head over and over about it. I'm just here to meet you. You're not what I pictured at all. From what I remember in the papers, you're a little girl—not that I've seen pictures of you."

Jennifer and Dave sat with their hands on the table and smiled. I felt safe in the room.

"I was going to bake muffins," he said. "But they said no." Again, I noticed the pitch of his voice. It was light, airy.

"Thank you for the thought," I replied.

"The video camera," Jennifer said. "We want to ask how private each of you considers this conversation. Who you talk to and who you don't. I know, Sheldon, you spoke of feeling uncomfortable about telling a psychologist that you were doing this. I know, Carys, you've said there are people who don't need to know."

I didn't recall telling her that; maybe she'd picked up on something from my references to the extended family on my father's side, or maybe she was thinking of the many months it had taken for me to tell my family.

"So I'm wondering if it might be good to take just a moment to talk about expectations." *Doesn't she mean confidentiality?* I thought. Confidentiality is a funny thing. It's one thing to respect someone's privacy, but what if that has the unintended but very real consequence of silencing someone else's experience? I wasn't a practitioner here, so I wasn't bound by any professional codes. I was a human being experiencing my life. We had already agreed in the letters that we could tell whomever we wanted.

And if he was going to tell a psychologist working on behalf of the Correctional Service of Canada, which would have an impact on his release no matter what the restorative justice workers assured me, then surely I had no guarantee of confidentiality or privacy. That seemed to be their problem, not mine. I wanted the power to reclaim my story. Murder had so often silenced the least powerful in this room. I wanted to know my story, have access to my story, share my story, and I didn't want anyone in my way.

"For me," I said to him, "this is an event in my life. Some people I share with and some I don't, so I would expect the same of you. If there are particular pieces of information you don't want me to share with other people, tell me."

"I'm comfortable with anything you want to share," he said.

"Okay," I said.

"Hopefully it's vice versa," he said. "It was just that nothing has ever changed in the twenty years I've been here. Reports are cut and pasted from previous reports. I really wanted to show them I've done a lot of things and that I've changed."

As he spoke, I heard the desperation to tell his story, to defend his identity as a decent human being.

I wondered if he felt I had the same right.

He continued. "So I took a stand—this is how I've changed—and, you know, I had to give her examples. So one of the examples I gave was the process I am doing with you. I don't share too much with the CSC. I'll share with certain staff members." He pointed to his parole officer's office. "I've known her for thirty years. Before I was even incarcerated. I tried to share with another parole officer, but then she left. Then I got another parole officer, but she didn't really care. Everything is on the surface with these people."

"Our experience of it is ours," I said. "You can share with who you want."

"And this is for longer than just this moment," Jennifer said.

"What are you most hoping to accomplish by the end of the day?" Dave asked. He gave examples: asking questions, getting information, and talking about the impact of the crime.

"If you have questions, feel free," Sheldon said. "If you have something on your mind, let me know. You'll get the truth."

"I would like to know what was going on in your life right before you came to our house and over the next couple of days," I said. "And the trial, I'm curious to know your experience of that."

"So, you want to hear about the day that I got arrested or the day that I got into your house?" he asked.

"The days before. What were you up to? You mentioned you moved to Calgary the year before."

"The fall before that."

"How old were you?"

"I was twenty-one when I came back from Winnipeg. Things didn't pan out. I was living with a girl. She was working for Greyhound. She gave me a ticket. Said, 'Get out of here, you asshole.' I didn't do nothing to her. I arrived home and rented a place underneath my uncle and lived there and worked until I got into a car accident in June. I broke my pelvis, smashed my face, and went to the hospital. The same place your dad was working. This is what I was told."

"Right."

"I was healing," he said. "Popping pills."

"What kind of pills?" I asked.

"Painkillers, narcotics. I built a tolerance. My doctor says, 'You've done way too much.' And I don't know if I was in pain or if it was mental pain because I lost my job. So I moved to my brother's, couldn't pay rent anymore, ran out of money. Then I started doing cocaine."

"Had you done those types of drugs before?"

"No. I played a little. Then it was just a spiral of drug abuse. Started doing B and E's on garages, took stuff like air compressors, and started selling it for dirt cheap to the work sites that I worked at. Then I'd go and get my drugs. And that's the way it was. Me and him, we'd been doing that for the longest time."

I knew he was referring to his friend, the guy who broke into garages with him, the guy whom he'd blamed for the murder.

"So one night we went to your garage, and there was a twin 280ZX in there. We were just going to take that. But I didn't know anyone to sell it to. We were going to drive it around—actually, it was just me. He wasn't even there."

I subtly cocked my head. Had he just lied? Twenty years after the crime, and that guy he blamed it on is still on his mind. Or had he come to our house before that night?

"I looked through the window," he said.

"Of the garage, first?" I asked.

"I looked through the window, tried the front door first."

It would have taken considerable effort to go from the front door of our home to the unlocked door of the garage in the back alley. Did he try the garage first, as he had just said, seeing my dad's car there? Or did he first try the front door of our home? These were very different stories, very important distinctions.

"I looked through the window of the basement, and I don't know if I seen something. Then I went around the back to the garage. I searched the car's glove compartment and found his key. I was just going to take the car and go off. Then I seen the window of the kitchen was open a little. So I went in through the kitchen window."

"What for?" I asked in a quieter voice. I stared at him, noting the inconsistencies—the clarifying, the backtracking.

"I have no idea. There's nothing that drove me to do that. It was just, uh…" He shook his head, then gestured with his hands as if to say, *There is no explanation for what I did.* "I thought I saw some—I don't even know, 'cause I could barely see inside. I just went inside, looked around, saw a bunch of coats on the racks. And I was going to try to get them all together, and I thought I heard something. So I grabbed the knife, and I went upstairs and investigated."

He picked up the knife after he heard the noise. Why did he pick up a knife? Why did he go upstairs? I wondered these things, but I didn't want to interrupt his train of thought.

"Then your dad stood up and came down the stairs, and then, um, when, uh…" He paused. I noticed his face became tense, like tears were building behind his eyes.

"You can slow down if you'd like," I told him.

"He was yelling something. I had made it down the stairs, and because my pelvis was still—I was slower. I was twenty-two, and I was in pretty good shape. The drugs that I was using, and my pelvis, slowed me down."

"What was he yelling?"

"He was angry. As he caught me, my head went into something." He gestured with his hand, hitting his head.

I remembered the wall just past the end of the stairs, covered in my father's blood.

"It took my cap right off, and I took the knife and went like this—" He made a fist, as though holding the knife as he had twenty years ago, and lifted it above his head. "And I got him right here." He pointed to his neck. "And then we were still struggling, and I went like this." He swung his hand to his right side, behind him. "And then I got him right here." He pointed to his waist. "And he still didn't leave me alone, and I went like this." He swung his hand to the side of his lower leg. "The knife broke on his shin, and he dropped, and I ran out."

I couldn't believe he was acting out the crime in front of me, performing it just a few feet away. My eyes widened in awe, feeling my father's body reacting in pain. I wondered, was it possible to stab someone at those angles while not facing him? Why was he recreating this violent act in front of me?

"And I didn't know. I honestly didn't know until the next day." He put his hands up in surrender.

"Did you leave out the front door?" I asked.

"I left out the front door."

"Which way did you go?"

He closed his eyes tightly. "I jumped a fence in the back alley."

But how could he have left through the front door and made it to the back alley? Did he jump our fence or someone else's? It didn't make sense.

"Then I ran down the street to the Stadium Shopping Centre. Where the Mac's store was," he continued.

"Yeah, I used to go there for candy with my friends," I said. And I used to go there with my father. This was my community. Where I lived my life, where everything changed. He changed the meaning of the homes, the stores, the streets. That was my neighbourhood, and he took it all away.

"Then I phoned a cab, gave them my name. Gave the driver eleven bucks and went home and just sat there wondering what I had done. Then I found out the next morning that it was your dad. Looked at my brother, who looked at me, and he knew exactly what was going on. I confessed everything. Right from day one. They came to my home. Then I went."

"Can we just pause for a moment," I said, more like a statement than a question. "I remember our garage and our backyard and our house. I'm assuming you were in the alley when you saw my dad's car. Was the garage open?"

"Yeah, the garage was open. We didn't kick nothing in. Well, I didn't kick anything in or make any noise."

He kept saying "we." Was this a consequence of lying for fifteen years? "Had you ever been to our house before?" I asked.

"Never. I'd never been to that area. That was the first I'd been to that area. I thought, because the area was a little more upscale than where I lived, there'd be better things."

Better cars, better jackets, more money to steal. When my father stood between him and the possessions he wanted to pawn, my life was thrown into chaos. For a jacket. For money. For things.

"From what I was looking at"—*in the garage in our backyard*, I thought as he spoke—"there was the car. That was it. Some tools thrown about." He took in a deep breath and exhaled loudly.

"Did that make you think there were things in my house, maybe?"

"Probably. I don't know what my mindset was as I went into the house." He paused. "It wasn't my MO to go into houses. Garages and only garages. I don't know if it was because I was alone that night. If I wasn't alone, he'd probably tell me to just go. I don't know what possessed me."

"When you looked through the windows, did you see people?"

"No, I didn't see anybody. That's probably why I went in. I didn't have a flashlight. I didn't have any tools to break into no houses. The tool that I got to open up the window to get in was a screwdriver that I found in your guys's garage."

"He had a lot of tools. He made a lot of things," I said. "Okay. Just one second." I looked around. "So when—in the letter you mention that you don't know why you just didn't leave when you heard voices. I'm assuming that they were my parents' voices?"

"I heard noise, rustling movement of some kind. Everything happened too fast that there wasn't no time. There was time where I thought to myself"—he put both hands up into the air—"let's just go, I don't know why I did what I did. I don't know why I went into your home. It was solely for financial gain. That was the only reason. I didn't want to leave empty-handed."

I nodded. I breathed.

"How do you feel?" he asked me.

"I feel shockingly fine. Like part of me is expecting to hear something that I don't know, or that surprises me." I paused. "The window you looked into was where my brother was sleeping."

"The bottom one," he said.

"He never slept down there again."

"No, I ..." he muttered and stopped.

"There were a lot of people in there."

I stroked my right hand with my left, resigned to the fact that the simplest of reckless, selfish decisions had changed our lives entirely. I was reimagining our family's younger selves, experiencing terror in our own home.

"My dad was a very strong man." I wiped the tears that were gathering beneath my eyes. "He was very strong."

Dave interjected. "So when you say your dad was strong, was he quite physically powerful as well?"

"All of it," I said. I didn't like that he'd interrupted my train of thought, the flow of questions.

"He was a big guy, very strong," Sheldon said.

Did he consider my father's strength some kind of self-defense, an excuse?

"He was a very athletic person," I said. "Not strong in an unusual way. He was beautiful and strong. Strong enough to sail a boat around the world." I paused. "You can continue."

"Did you turn yourself in at that point?" Dave asked him.

"I waited. I didn't know what to do. I didn't fall asleep. I didn't go home and crash out. I went home and stayed up the whole night and waited until my brother got up, and we just sat there. He goes, 'Where were you last night?' and I just told him. He said, 'I figured you'd do something stupid.' When I left your house, I prayed and I prayed, *Don't let him die, Don't let him die.* That's why I have no faith. You know what I mean?" He looked up at the ceiling, motioned his hands upward.

"Did you have faith before?" I asked.

"You know, I thought someone was looking out for me. Considering I should have died in that car accident. You see, I went to a Ride for Sight."

"Sorry, a what?"

"A Ride for Sight, for blind people. It's a rally. Kind of a deal for bikers and stuff. My friends invited me."

After that, he said he got a call from a friend whom he hadn't seen in a while. His friend gave him an address, telling him to come to a barbecue to have a few drinks. So he went. They then decided to go out and while driving, one of their car's wheels came off. The tow truck arrived and took him home. After that, he went out again, taking his girlfriend's car this time. They went to meet some people, had a few more beers, and hopped into his girlfriend's car after the bars closed.

"I think I had too much to drink," he said. "Shouldn't have been driving. Jumped into the vehicle, and the front tire was flat. So I grabbed the donut in the back and put it on the front. I was going off Deerfoot Trail and bam, a truck hit me. Crushed us on the driver's side like a tin can. My friend was ejected. We went to the hospital. I was unconscious."

I wasn't entirely sure why he was going into the minute details of an event that had occurred three months before he came to our house. But I could sense the calm before the storm.

"I wasn't—didn't even know anything about your dad. The only time I found out about your dad was after I murdered him. I went to the hospital during my thirty-day assessment. I had a couple of friends who worked at the hospital, and they'd come up through the security door, where you have to swipe your card, to visit me. They were concerned. But they put up a bunch of red flags for the nurses, who said my friends had to leave."

I recalled how the investigators tried to prove that some employees at the hospital had given him my father's address. They couldn't prove it, but they'd interviewed some offenders in prison at the time.

"Came back a couple of days later, and the nurses asked, 'Did you know that doctor?' I said, 'No.' They said, 'He was the doctor that treated you in June. When you had that car accident.'"

As soon as he said that, I realized it was what he'd been waiting to tell me all along, to let me know their paths had crossed before that night. My focus zoomed in on him. Everything was quiet, except for his voice.

"And that was the first time I found out it was your dad. Of course my heart sank. I knew I wasn't going to get a good assessment." He laughed sarcastically. "Like I said, someone was looking out for me that night. I should have called it quits and gone home. But what drove me was people wanting to be around me. That was the first time I'd heard about your dad."

"Yeah, I don't know what that would have been like, in the hospital," I said. "My dad was quite well known."

"Someone had told me that the officers wanted to take blood from me while I was on the table. To find out if I'd been drinking. And your dad told them to get out of there. Basically, 'You're not touching him. Leave him alone.' So he kind of saved me from getting a charge as well." He laughed again.

I laughed too, but ironically. If my dad hadn't cared for him, hadn't treated him with dignity, who knows where we'd be today? "That's exactly what my dad would do. That's him," I said. He would have looked at this stupid young boy in trouble, and he would have cared.

"'Don't touch him. You ain't touching him.' That's what I was told he said. And the next couple of days he'd come in, and—I think it was him. Asked if I was doing all right, and that was it. I don't remember all that much. I did have some kind of trauma."

"But you remember being cared for by him?" I clarified this in part because I remembered in his previous letters he'd said he didn't remember him at all. In fact, I recalled that he said he was unconscious the entire time. I wished I had brought the letter so I could show him his own words. The discrepancies were everywhere, and yet I didn't call him out on them.

I knew in my heart that this untrustworthy man was so fragile, so precarious that I would need to just listen to what he said and come to my own conclusions about what was going on. I'd read his words, his slow disclosures of information, and I realized that it would happen now, as I sat across from him: he would tell me that he did, in fact, remember my father.

"He'd come and check on me. He checked me out of the hospital, as far as I know. I said, 'I'm kind of ready to get out of here,' broken pelvis and all. And, um ... I think it was him. He was a tall man, dark hair, as far as I remember.'"

Anyone could find a photo of him, I thought. "So you do remember being cared for by him?" I asked, emphasizing that he did remember, despite having written that he didn't. "Do you remember his style, his personality?" Sheldon could have memorized my father's facial features, but I wanted to know, did he remember my father's way of being?

"He wasn't soft-spoken. He was hip. Do you know what I mean? He smiled. I don't know if he adapted the way he spoke to people. He was like, um—"

"Sounds like he was cool," Dave said. I looked at him, surprised that he was interrupting this flow of information that Sheldon had never shared before. I refocused my gaze on Sheldon. As far as I was concerned, it was just him and me in the room.

"He was cool. Yeah. He wasn't stoic or gritty. He was, 'How are you doing, there?' Cool cat, as far as I can remember. He spoke to me like it mattered. You know what I mean? Like there was some caring. Like some doctors come in and say, 'What's your problem?' He went that extra step, that's how I felt. I do remember that."

I wiped tears away with a tissue. I was in awe, not of his accurate description of my father, but that they had met each other before Sheldon came to our house. They'd interacted. My father had made an impression on him, as he had on so many other people, and Sheldon remembered the interaction as distinctive.

Right then, I got it—I knew that Sheldon knew what he'd taken away.

"That's exactly how my father was described," I said. "Whether it was his kid or friend or patient—a lot of patients came to the memorial services—they'll tell you that. Exactly what you're looking for in a doctor. That's what he was like. And you'll see that in all of us. In my family."

A clarity suddenly came over me. My body relaxed as it had never done before. "I had no idea you had a conversation with him," I continued. "That actually makes me feel better." I had finally confirmed he'd had a glimpse, a real-life glimpse, of what he had taken away from me.

"He made me sign a waiver," he said. "Like, he wanted to keep me in, and I said, 'No, I don't want to stay here.' So he said, 'You have to sign your way out. I'll get the nurse for you. You're on your own.'"

"Did you recognize him on the news?" I asked.

"No. Like I said, when I was in the hospital people were coming in and out. There were other doctors checking in too. I do remember him. But I don't remember him well. Like, he was not my family doctor. He was just an emergency doctor that night, and that was the night I met him. I had no idea where I was going, and it shocked me to the core when I found out."

"That would do it," I said.

"And then it just became 'I don't want to be the guy that committed this crime.' So I came up with this big scheme with my friend, and it didn't pan out. I told him what had happened and read an excerpt from the Criminal Code and told him that if he said it at my trial, we could both get off. I wanted there to be enough reasonable doubt to say that I didn't do it. He said no the day before we went to trial. So I went into self-survival mode and tried to raise reasonable doubt myself. It didn't pan out. I got convicted. The jury didn't like it at all."

"I'm curious to know what counsel you had," I said.

"This was his first murder trial. I had confessed everything to a lawyer before him. And because of confidentiality, he couldn't say nothing. But I said, 'I did it. I'm sorry that I did it. What can we do?' And he said, 'There's not much I can do for you. We can present it to the courts, and the courts will decide whether you'll get life or not. And most likely you'll get life.'"

"The first guy told you that?" I asked, getting confused between his two lawyers.

"So, 'You're fired.' And I had to come up with another plan. That's what happened. Otherwise I would have gone in and said, 'Yeah,' to the courts. And I should have."

"*Yes*," I said.

"Yes." He looked down. "For sure." He paused. "Life is life, no matter if it's seven years or twenty-five years. I was told in the remand centre, 'You're going to be in there until they decide to let you out.' I didn't want that. I didn't want to be here until I was old and grey. I barely lived a life myself." He added, "That's not a pity party for me."

"No, I wouldn't let you do that," I said.

Dave looked at me. "It sounds like he's telling you why he resisted."

"Yeah, of course." I understood why Sheldon was telling me all this. Shame had fuelled the lies. "Why would you ever want to be known as the person who killed my father?" Clearly I understood, but it didn't make it right.

"So you go from a guy who breaks into garages and steals compressors to the guy who commits this crime," Dave said.

"I didn't want to be that guy. I couldn't look in my mom's eyes and tell her. She came to visit. I said, 'It wasn't me, Mom.' My brother, I told him. But she wanted to hear it from me. I eventually told everyone what I did."

I wondered whom he included in "everyone." Because he had not told me. He'd waited until I contacted him.

"It's strange what you hear as an eleven-year-old," I said. "You have no way of fact-checking. Even at the trial. Was it two weeks, the actual trial?"

"It was the Stampede," he said, meaning the famous Calgary Stampede.

"I was sent to camp. My sisters got a babysitter, and my brother and I went to camp. I had no clue there was a trial going on."

"Are you mad they kept you in the dark?" he asked.

"I'm more focused on the mini injustices afterward, like not having access to information. The world doesn't grasp that kids grow up and want to process it all. We were being protected from a lot of things, me and my family."

But I found the protection to be condescending and paternalistic, as though I couldn't handle what was going on. I hated when information was being kept from me. I hated that I didn't have access to the truth. I hated that we children were thought incapable of understanding what was going on, when in reality we had an uncanny ability to comprehend. "I'm mad at what gets to be said and what doesn't," I finally said.

"Me too," he said.

The rest of the morning flew by. He spoke about the future. "I'll likely stay in Drumheller. Maybe I'll be a mechanic where I work." He spoke about taking courses at a nearby college: "I have some trades I can do. But I'm too old and too fat to be a heavy-duty mechanic. I'll do something small. With a trade, I can go anywhere."

"Where do you want to go?" I asked.

"I have no idea what I'm going to do. First get college done, then decide. Try to make some money. But I don't know where."

"I'll likely be notified by letter," I said. "I won't know a street address, but I'll know the city."

"To take the courses, I'll need permission. A year of work and then go to school. I know what I'm doing. I fix the engines for the tractors and lawn mowers. It's something I like to do." He pointed to the shop outside. "That's my job."

I expressed curiosity about his journey through the different prisons. It started at a maximum-security institution in Edmonton. He was labelled a snitch by other prisoners there because he pinned the crime on someone else. "I took to the hole, forty-five days" the first time. The prisoners left a note for him: *We'll stab you if you don't leave.* He was then shipped off to a prison in New Brunswick, where he stayed from 1995 to 1998. In 1999, he went back to Boden, in Edmonton. "I was still in with my girlfriend, but in 2002 I broke up with her and came here, in 2003, to Drumheller," he said. He was still trying the Court of Appeal, "so I couldn't cop to what I'd done that night." He said he hadn't been eligible to take his case to the Supreme Court.

"I told a psychologist at the Regional Psychiatric Centre in Saskatoon, in 2004," he said. "Everything started changing as soon as I got it off my chest. I told everyone."

Again I thought, *He didn't tell me. He didn't tell my family.*

"My family started talking more. I stopped doing drugs," he said.

"How did you get drugs into the prison?" I asked.

"My girlfriend brought drugs to me. You can make quadruple the amount in jail. A bale of tobacco goes for five hundred dollars here, twenty on the street. You can make all kinds of money. Drugs were a way to stay alive rather than to get high. I wasn't using any hard stuff, just marijuana. If I had the dope, no one would touch me. It's how I survived. But the animosity carries on to this day. How I lied—blaming someone else for the crime. I carry the snitch label. When someone sees that show, *Exhibit A,* the prisoners feed off it."

He was talking about the TV docudrama series that re-enacts how criminal cases are solved using forensic science. One episode used my family's crime as the storyline, how smudged prints and gloves helped to get the conviction.

"It's a feeding frenzy. There are gossipers, whisperers. I was attacked in the gym about a year ago. So I keep my mouth shut. I've been drug-free since 2005. There's marijuana everywhere. I think alcohol is worse than marijuana. It destroys relationships. I won't use anymore. Coffee, that's about it. It's not hip to me, maybe because I'm forty-two."

I thought about his age. I thought about his eventual release date, and how close he'd be to the age my father was when he died.

"It was my choice to go to the Regional Psychiatric Centre. There are very nice people there."

"It's a supportive environment," Jennifer said.

"The social workers, they make you feel important. They have empathy. Jennifer is another person—bonus. That centre, it's more of a treatment centre. Equipped from max to minimum. You're treated like human beings. Here, you're alone. You're left to your own devices. Even the way they treat medical needs. I had a slipped disc in my back, and there was a suspicion that I just wanted narcotics. I had emergency surgery after a long time waiting for an X-ray." He paused. "Have you been back to Calgary?" he asked me.

"We moved to Vancouver after that school year ended," I said. "After his memorial, we came back home to Calgary. We stayed in a hotel for a bit," referring to the time when our house was being cleaned. All the carpets were replaced, and all the walls were painted. Everything looked different. But one of our family friends made sure that the doorframe to the kitchen stayed unpainted because it had the yearly markings of our heights scratched into the wood.

"We come back. I visit friends, family friends. Seeing Calgary as an adult is different. After my dad died, a lot of community members put money into a fund to support our schooling, to go to university. In the mid-2000s we came back and gave the remaining funds to our old elementary school. The librarian bought books. The music room bought a piano. I went to university in Victoria. Did a lot of school. I don't know if I'll go back to school. I like to work."

"So you work with kids right now?" he asked.

I nodded. "Teaching, too. Slowly getting into that. Like my mom. She's been an instructor since I was born."

"Your mom was a lawyer at one point in time, no?"

"No, but she has a law and political science degree from the UK. She teaches people to assist lawyers."

"Your mom is a compassionate person. She wrote to the Parole Board a few times. Kind of forgiving, I guess. I was surprised. I am surprised by you guys."

"What do you mean?"

"Just the compassion, that's all. Night and day between you and your uncles, I can tell you that. But I expect that. I've had it all my life. I never expected this, ever, to sit across the table. Like when my name got called today. I was really nervous, not so much now. I'm happy about the process. We've been writing and stuff, and it's just, like, something that I never thought would happen. You know what I mean?"

"It's not something that happens a lot," Jennifer said.

"Fifteen thousand prisoners across Canada," Dave said.

"There are a lot of victims out there, a lot of animosity," Sheldon said. "Not everyone is happy about being a victim of crime. I'm not saying you're happy, it's just"—he corrected himself—"for you to seek it out, it's commendable, I guess."

"We were cared for by our mom's family," I said. "It was the littlest things. Buying us mattresses. Driving us around, so many of us. They're teachers and nurses and social workers, a whole bunch of women. For better or for worse, my mom asks, 'How can we all move forward?' Her coping strategy doesn't allow you to struggle, but it allows you to move forward and not be super angry.

"One of the reasons I wanted to do this," I continued, "is that writing to you is the opposite. I want to acknowledge that you were—are—a part of our lives. Once when I was talking to a friend and she asked about you, I realized that I had a limited window of time to have control over this process. That's when I found Dave and his team."

"What did you tell them about me at the time?" Sheldon asked.

"Nothing. Just the age you were when you killed my dad. That was hugely significant to me."

"Why?"

"Because when I got to that age, I was just starting my profession. I had a lovely life, I was learning lots, and I had wonderful friends. I asked myself, *Why am I sitting in my residence room, getting ready to go to school with lovely people? And why, at the same age as me, did you break into our house?*" Tears started running down my face as I spoke. "It was fascinating to reflect on it, at that time. I was thinking last night that you're now near the age when my dad died, and I find that interesting as well. I get reflective. I don't know if you do that. It's just a thing I do."

"I live more in the moment," he said. "My reflections on the past are all terrible, so I try to focus on my future. I don't forget. I have a good memory of what I've been through. It's nice to see a different perspective from you. To know how you guys feel about it. It's tough for me. I've done a lot of crying about it, shed a lot of tears. It's like your perspective is different than what I'd get from an angry point of view. I'm used to that one, your uncles' side. Not this one." He pointed to me. "It's sometimes overwhelming. I don't want to see you cry. So you might as well stop that right now," he said jokingly.

"Sometimes it's easier to feel anger than to feel pain. I can't claim to know my family's experience, but I do know mine." I paused, considering how to say it. I wanted him to know that it wasn't just trauma he brought into my world—it was being scared, never feeling safe, never sure your world is not going to crumble into pieces again.

"You took away the joy," I blurted out. "Twenty years later, we only have moments of joy. That's what went away. We were a lovely family, and there was a lot of joy. My dad embodied this. That's just the tip of the iceberg, how you described him. He brought a lot of life into the room. Into the relationship with my mom. And just everything—that went away." Just like that. I gulped hard. "I think all our journeys have been to re-create that. And, man, that's fucking hard." I smiled, wiping more tears from my face. "But it's quite nice when you get to feel it again.

"A lot of people have a lot of ideas as to how we should get better," I continued. "But I don't like any of their ideas. The coolest thing that can come out of this is to still have a relationship with my dad. Not in a sad way, but in an everyday type of way. That's been how I get through it."

"It's like they have a script they go by," he said. "Different people have different views on things."

"We went to counsellors who told us lots of things, told us what to do. And we just wanted them to say that what each of us was feeling was okay."

"You were precocious," Dave said. "You both feel that condescension. You both mention experiencing empathy." He looked at me. "It will make you a good teacher."

"I'm not surrounded by that," Sheldon said. "At the Psychiatric Centre was the only time. That's what made me, you know what I mean, come out. If you had come ten years earlier," he said, looking at me, "I would have told you right there."

I wondered if that was true.

"I've been in an environment where I've felt safe telling someone how I feel or what I've done. You know what I mean? It's like a breath of fresh air. I'm not accustomed to it."

"When I get a sense of what my uncles feel, I hate that feeling. When I am around them, I want to throw up."

"I just want to hide, stick my head in a hole," he said. "I enjoyed reading your letters, theirs not so much."

"I stay away," I said, wondering, *Maybe it's taught me something.*

Maybe their anger taught me how to know what was right.

"They don't know you've come here?" he asked.

"Oh, God, no. They'd probably think that I'm dishonouring my father."

"A traitor," he said.

"They'd probably say, 'How dare you not be angry for the rest of your life.' But I can't take that. I just don't want to be anywhere around that."

"If I remember correctly, your mom didn't come with them either," he said.

"Oh, God, no," I said quickly.

"Your mom sat separately. She read her letter, was the first to go. Those guys read their letter like I was scum."

"What was their response to my mom's letter?" I asked.

"One of them said, 'Her views are different than what we have to say.' I'm not allowed to turn around to see them," he said. "Your mom was totally different, and I appreciated it."

"I was debating going with her, but I decided not to. At that point, I had an idea that I wanted to make contact with you, but I didn't want it under someone else's terms. That environment would make me feel awful. Then I began to wonder about what I could do under my terms."

"We've seen people do parole hearings and then do this the next day, and they can't believe the difference," Dave said.

"It's quarter after eleven now. You guys want to go for lunch?" Jennifer asked.

"Can you recommend somewhere?" I asked Sheldon.

"The Vintage is good." He gave us directions. "You can talk about me if you want," he joked.

"You wish," Jennifer said.

"I'll see you," he said, and left the room.

Upon moving back to Vancouver, her mother asks her parents to take over their family tradition: report card dinners. Each school term, her grandparents take her, her siblings, and her mother out to dinner. Doing well at school is the most important achievement. She knows that from the stories, the conversations, and the rewards.

Her mother tells of the adventures she had after high school, travelling to the UK to complete her undergraduate degree. She tells of her grandparents' adventures after World War II and going to the UK where her grandfather completed school on a Rhodes scholarship. And her father had travelled to New Zealand to do his medical residency after his training at the University of British Columbia. She wonders what she'll do when she reaches the age when she'll go to university.

She does not always get straight-A report cards like her siblings, but she comes close enough. Besides, she thinks, school isn't just about grades.

"As and Bs, what's this?" her grandfather says jovially as they sit at the table. "The best I could do in grade school were Cs," he proclaims, which is exactly what her dad would say.

She looks at her report card after her grandparents hand it back to her. She thinks about her teachers, the ones who, day in and day out, are there to teach her something new when she arrives to class each day. She doesn't know what she would do if she didn't have her teachers.

WHAT MADE
THE DIFFERENCE

22

ennifer and Dave were asking me what I wanted to talk about this afternoon," I said to Sheldon when we returned after lunch. "I told them that I was really satisfied with what we talked about. We covered all of the pieces that I had wondered about. I've been trying to heal for twenty years, which is an ongoing journey. So I'm wondering what that journey looks like for you?"

"I'm definitely not going to play catch-up," he said. "My brother has a family. All my friends have grown-up families. I'm not going to try to get a girlfriend, procreate. I just got to focus on what I do, my schooling, day by day. Hopefully I'll have a roof over my head. I have no grand scheme. My days will be long and boring, and I'll be under the radar for the rest of my life. I might do some fishing. Might join a band. It depends. Did I tell you about my family?"

"Sounds like it was first a connection, then a disconnection," I said.

"Yeah, it's not going to be good. I'll be on my own. Won't be an easy road. But before I came to jail, I was living on my own from an early age. I never connected with them anyway. Everything that I've done, they blame me for. I want to meet new people. Once you get to know me, I'm all right, I guess. I hope," he laughed. "It's going to be a struggle. I want to focus on school and work."

"School saved my life," I said. "If I didn't have school every day and my teachers, who took my mind off things ... It was a huge piece of my own healing. Which is probably why I stayed in it so long."

"That's all I want to do, work hard and live normal, if I can. No big schemes. No big plans. When you make a five-year plan—No, I don't know what I'm doing in five days."

"You mentioned a band," Jennifer said.

"I'm the musician around here," he responded.

"What kinds of music do you listen to?" I asked.

"Everything," he said.

"How do you access it?" I wondered.

"I don't have a computer. I have to buy CDs—that's probably ancient for you. I've got about five hundred albums. Collected them. Saved up a little money to buy one here and there. We're not allowed music players or cell phones. I don't even know what a cell phone looks like."

"It keeps changing," I said.

"The last computer I saw had a green screen and floppy discs." Everyone laughed.

"I really appreciate you writing to me," I said.

"Me too," he said.

"Before we started this, it was kind of a mystery, who you were," I said. "So you were more of a ghost. There was this person who affected our lives, but we didn't talk about that. I've appreciated you just being a person, and that I could be a person to you as well."

"I didn't want you to think I was this huge monstrous man who broke into your home. I wanted you to see I'm a normal guy. If you go to the population down here, there are a lot of scary dudes. I don't know if you had a picture in mind. But I wanted to put you at ease, which is why I sent you that picture. I asked people, too, 'Should I or should I not?' One person said, 'Send her a picture.' I said, 'Well, I don't know how she'll take it.' She said, 'Yeah, just send it.'"

"I don't have an adult version of then," I said. "So I have no idea what my mom visualizes and how she's integrated that into her mind. I've never envisioned you that way. It's more like a ghost or like nothing. I have a lot of other images from that night that I've had to respond to. I chose not to look at the picture. Seeing you was a part of meeting you."

"I thought you were just a little girl with pigtails. All I've ever imagined. I have a picture of your dad. Of your grandmother and her sons. From the impact statement at the parole board. He's standing in a jean shirt, longer hair, a smoke in his mouth, wearing a watch, and looking sideways. That's the only picture. And I have your mom's impact statement. I just went through all of that."

As he mentioned the documents, it reminded me of something I had wanted to ask. "There are a lot of administrative documents," I said. "One of the pieces was something to do with the end of the trial—a summarized statement, maybe a sort of decision commentary from the judge. I was informed that you might have a summary of the end of the trial."

"Reasons for Judgment, a sentencing overview," Jennifer clarified.

"I have all of the transcripts. Decision of my appeal. Summations. Check the law library underneath 1992, and you'll see my name there in the law books. Gives you everything," Sheldon said.

"I'm interested in the judge's summary at the end of the trial."

"He went on and on," he said. "After the guilty verdict, they sent the jury away again for sentence recommendations. And they sentenced me right there. He told my lawyer and the prosecution that they did a good job. He said something to your family and sent the jury away." He paused and I wondered why he was telling me what happened when I had asked for the document, not his recollection. I listened.

"Then he asked me if I had anything to say. I said something—I can't remember—something about my life. He proceeded to—" Sheldon's hands tightened. "He started to go off at me about something. I zoned out. I don't remember, to be honest. 'Guilty.' I zoned out.

"I dug my own grave. I should have just said, 'Yes, it was me.' But even if I'd gotten away with it, even if I was found not guilty, I don't know what I'd be doing with myself. 'Cause I know what I did. So I don't know where I'd be today."

"It would be helpful for her to have the documents," Jennifer said. I was glad that she'd repeated my request, because he'd gone off on another tangent.

"Even though the internet is a vast place, it's hard to know what to look for," I said.

"You and I can look for it," Jennifer said to Sheldon.

"I'll see what I can do," he replied.

"Thank you."

"It's not very nice, though," he said.

"I would imagine."

"So, while not pleasant, it is another piece of that history," Jennifer said.

"Is there anything else you were wanting to know?" I asked.

"We pretty much covered it," Sheldon said. "No, I'm tired."

"You've covered a lot of ground," Jennifer said.

"I've settled a lot of my fears today," he said. "I feel your pain. I don't want you to think I'm cold hearted."

"You're not coming across that way."

"I'm not used to this kind of interaction. I'm used to on-the-surface kinds of stuff. This is pretty deep. You're brave for dealing with it. I'm happy that we've met. I don't know how you've felt about it. Do you want to keep this conversation going? It's up to you."

"I appreciate that. I'll want to go back and reflect, and I'll be writing to you soon. I have no clue after that. I think it would be odd to meet you and to never have contact again. But I don't know what that looks like. The past year, I only wrote when I wanted to, when I was well and safe. I had a concrete view of the next few months, of writing. And then I knew I wanted to meet you. But from now on, I don't know.

"I wrote my letters because you wrote your letters. If I don't receive a letter from you, you won't receive a letter from me. I don't want to overstep my boundaries."

"Thank you."

"So you'd like a response." Jennifer looked at me.

"Yes, and I'm sure we could discuss that. We both hopefully have a lot of years yet to live."

"I hope," he said. "I feel more comfortable writing letters, too. I can express myself better. Because I can think about my thoughts. It's totally up to you."

"I would expect that, a response from you," I said.

"I like to instantly respond, so you'll get it soon after."

"So this was good?" Sheldon asked.

"Yes," I responded.

"Me too."

Dave jumped in. "Not wanting to re-engage in some beginning place, Carys, but at lunch you said that you wanted to find out about the time Sheldon began telling the truth, what made the difference." He looked at Sheldon. "Sheldon, you mentioned something about empathy."

I recalled our conversation at lunch an hour before. Dave and Jennifer asked me if there was anything that I wanted to clarify from our conversation thus far, or ensure we covered something in particular before we left. Sitting in the pub near our hotel, I reflected, silently. I told them that if I forgot to ask, I wanted to know why he began telling the truth after more than a decade of lying.

I looked at Sheldon. "What was the thing that made the difference?" I asked.

"A lovely woman, Ellen." He began to describe what seemed to be a social worker or counsellor who facilitated their group counselling sessions. "She made me feel so comfortable. I wouldn't tell anyone because I have no trust, because every time there'd be a confrontation right after. I was afraid I'd be attacked, you know. So it got to a point that I'm not telling CSC anything because sooner or later it'll get out. When I finally did get to the Psychiatric Centre in Saskatoon, Ellen presented herself to me. She said, 'You need to tell me what you need to tell me.' I felt it was time, because I felt safe. There'd be no leak. No judgment. Nothing like that. And did I let it flow! Everything came out. It was like a cancer bringing me down. I certainly did come clean. Night and day."

"Why did you feel safe with her?" Jennifer asked.

"Just the way she was. Compassionate about everything, like 'You come to me if you need anything.' I felt more comfortable in a one-on-one setting. I'm not going to blurt out that I blamed it on someone else in a group setting. It was time for me to move on, to find out why I did what I did. And in order to do that, I need to tell, not sugar-coat it. 'You did it, you've been living with it, and it's time to come clean,' she said. And she made it easy for me. She took me out of that room and said, 'You've got something on your chest. We're going to do this once a week.' And then I came clean to everyone who mattered to me. In order for me to grow."

"You have some powerful observations here," Dave said.

"Well, I had to do something. I was using. I was getting into trouble. I was involved in three riots. It was like I never learned my lesson the first eight years. I was too bitter, too mad at myself about the hurt that I caused. I thought, *How am I going to get out of this mess?*"

Then he stopped himself. "This is like a parole board hearing. But I want you to know that I'm not that person, and I'll never be that person again, because I know the damage that I caused. I'll never do that again. And I'm sorry it happened. I've beaten myself up enough for it—and I can take a good punch."

I sat back, leaning into the chair, and felt overwhelmed. I felt my father's presence in me, a compassion so strong.

"I think my dad would say, 'Go live your life. Do what you're good at. Do what makes you feel alive instead of what kills you inside.' Yes, I think he would say that."

"That's all I needed to hear," he said. "I just—" He paused. "I've never had that before."

"How does it feel to you to have Carys say this?" Dave asked.

"It would have been nice to have a good kick in the butt a long time ago," he said.

Then I felt it, just as Jennifer had assured me that morning I would.

"Now I'm done," I said clearly, confidently. "Earlier, I didn't shake your hand because I thought that physical contact would be overwhelming and would interfere with the present moment. This is the most awkward thing in the world, but I would like to shake your hand as a part of the process, to thank you for meeting with me."

Everyone stood up. I approached him, stood a few feet away, and extended my hand. He did the same. I felt his thick palm and callused skin, looked straight into his eyes, and said, "Thank you very much."

As we left the prison grounds and headed to the airport to see if we could catch an earlier flight, I stared into the open fields, my head resting against the passenger door window.

I thought to myself, *I've just met my father's murderer. And if I can meet my father's murderer, then I can do anything.* It was as though the confidence that had been ripped from my soul twenty years before had re-entered my body throughout the day. I felt it build in me. An absence I had not noticed, I only recognized its presence. Drenched in the prairie light, in contrast to the darkness of the night before, I felt the confidence rightfully, pridefully, calmly returning.

Jennifer dropped us off at the airport. As I stared into the blurred horizon of kiosks, bars, tables, and chairs, I ignored Dave's chatter. I was exhausted. I checked my phone and saw my sisters' and friends' text messages, which had accumulated throughout the day. *Call me if you need. Thinking of you. Here if you need me.* What a gift. Their support warmed me. Even though they knew I wasn't going to call, they were there, and that's all I needed. I'd pushed them out of my mind so I could be present throughout the day, yet they'd been concerned about me the whole time.

As we flew from Calgary to Abbotsford, I started wondering about the healing effects of gaining a voice when everything around you demands silence. Silence can be a violent thing.

It was dark by the time I returned home. Through my window overlooking English Bay, I saw the lights of nearby ships scatter on the water's surface. I dropped my bags at the door and headed to my bedroom. After I let my clothes fall to the floor, I got into my bed and wrapped a sheet around myself, and soon I was asleep.

She looks at her course schedule in early September, goes to her guidance counsellor. "I won't be able to get through grade twelve without my math teacher," she says, knowing she needs to be able to see her every other day.

She sits in planning class looking at her favourite photograph of her father, having completed the assigned activity before the allocated time is up. Her teacher doesn't say a thing, just squeezes her shoulder as he walks by her desk.

She takes photographs of her backyard, of the cliffs and the ocean behind her house, then returns to school to develop the film in the lab.

Every day, she arrives early to school and leaves late, looking forward to being with people who welcome her.

PART SIX:

MEETING
HEAD-ON

*When two power vessels are approaching head on, both vessels
should alter course to starboard to pass port-side to port-side.*
—National Maritime College

23
MOURNING BREAKS

Tell me everything," Shannon said. We had positioned ourselves on the grass in the park near her work—my old workplace.

"I told him that my dad made you feel like you were the most important person in the room," I said. "He loved everyone. He found everyone interesting. I told him that that's what he took away."

Shannon looked at me attentively and said, "That's what your dad gave you."

Only when she said this did it occur to me how deeply true this was. I'd never lose that. I looked at Shannon. "He would have really liked you."

Later that week, I sent a short message to Katy, the woman from Victoria I'd originally contacted before any of this started, and let her know I'd met with Sheldon with the help of the same restorative justice workers who'd supported her journey. I told her that I felt like a better person because of it and thanked her for being there in spirit. She replied soon thereafter, telling me that she had read my email on the beach, which inspired her to lay back on the sand and listen to the waves lapping peacefully at the shore.

The account of that day had a different effect on some other friends, however.

"Oh, he totally came to your house on purpose," one friend said, fixated on that one act.

"Do you think he's lying?" I asked, then immediately regretted the question. Because if the police, lawyers, and I had no way of finding out, neither would anyone else.

As one friend said this, and then another, I felt a wrenching in my gut. I hadn't questioned him in the meeting because I'd gone along with how I felt in that moment. It wasn't my focus. But now, I found myself questioning the authenticity of his words. By the end of the week, I was questioning everything. Whether I had conveyed to him that I believed him, when I didn't entirely believe. Whether I was naïve to believe there was a chance he was telling the truth after so many years of lying. These doubts stewed in my head for days.

I sent a note to Dave and Jennifer asking them if they thought he was withholding information. I assured them that I wasn't changing my impressions of the day, but that I wondered if he would continue reveal more information, and if that might include, at last, why he had chosen our house.

Jennifer replied, *I truly don't know.*

> In many ways I'm not sure what he has to gain from withholding, but of course, he may see things differently. There is always the possibility that it is still something he has not been able to come to terms with or that he sees as a risk of some sort. I don't imagine, whether or not he had chosen the house, that his sentence or parole chances would have changed much if at all, given the length of his sentence already, but that doesn't mean he wouldn't perceive a risk.

She said she was open to asking him questions to clarify, if I wanted.

When I read her response, I appreciated its neutrality but had to remind myself of her role as a facilitator, not an investigator of truth. I got a sense that this lingering question wasn't on their radar. They had no idea of its history and importance, how it had irked my family and everyone who knew my father. I realized that I would have to deal with this by myself.

The police and lawyers couldn't prove it. There were inconsistencies across the board. Did he come to our house on purpose or not? Who could I trust? Who would tell me what exactly had happened that night?

The questions circulated and gained power, so much so that when the next friend asked "How did it go?" all I could say was, "Do you mind if we don't talk about it?"

I stopped talking about it. I held the questions close, to process them on my own, to decide what it all meant to me. The insights, the questions, and the terrors—they were all mine.

A month or so later, I waited in the lobby of the Granville Island Hotel where I was meeting my stepsister and her mother and stepfather for dinner. I recognized her stepfather as he approached.

"I guess we're the early ones," he said.

"As always."

We laughed and began a conversation, one that I assumed would stay superficial, given that he was my stepsister's stepfather.

"Hey, did you know that I knew your father?" he said, out of the blue.

"No, I didn't know that," I said, astonished at the thought.

"Well, I only met him a few times, in the sailing world. I met your mother and father before you were born, when they were out on a trip up the coast."

"No way!" I said. "I love meeting people who knew my father."

"Do you sail?"

"No. We used to sail all the time. We were out on the water every summer for at least a few weeks. My dad was trying to teach us how to sail. You should have seen my brother steering the dinghy. Freaked my mom right out. I just love being on the water."

"Do you ever consider getting back into it?"

"I don't even know how I'd begin!"

"Let me know if you need a contact sometime. You should take some lessons."

"I will. Thanks."

After my stepsister and her mother arrived and we had dinner together, we headed to a theatre space near the hotel for a poetry event.

"You girls are going to love this poet," my stepsister's mother said to us. "Just you wait."

Soon after, the poet Lemn Sissay walked onstage. A Brit of Ethiopian ancestry, a foster care-system survivor, a powerhouse of a gentle man, he soon had me mesmerized. It did not bother me that he spoke quickly, as I suffered from the same affliction. So much to say, I reasoned. Then he began "Mourning Breaks":

> They always said I was over the edge
> And now I am. I really am over the edge!
> But as I dropped in a gasp of air I grasped a branch.
> That, I hoped, had its roots in the rock or rock solid roots
> But there's a breeze blowing, a stunning storm coming
> Thickening ink spills and swills on a bleating paper sky
> A crowd of rain on the horizon staggers nearer
> I sway so. I know so. I slip a little more
> I know so I sway so. I grip a little more.
> These tender fingers in a clenched fist
> I must have slit my back. It hurts like a howl.
> It stings like a scowl, weeps and stings again.

The skin splitting and splitting from my spine sides

And a pain develops muscles that create mouths

That simulate sounds of whole cities screaming.

There's a storm coming. A coming storm.

Dust spits from the cliff top into my river-eyes

Forcing tears over the banks to flood me.

I will not drown in them. I will not drown.

I'm hanging on. I am hanging on. I am hanging on.

In the zip of a thick ribbon of wind

A god or a devil appears floating in front of me

And tells me in a hunch of a NY accent

"Let go, let go—Death is just the beginning

Of the end of the beginning of the end ..."

And continued for forty-one days and forty-one nights

"Of the end of the beginning of the end of the End ..."

And in a crack of lightning the devil or the god vanished.

Nothing more to concentrate on. But a storm

The sky. And my breaching back. And the cliff

And the edge. And the uprooting branch.

And my knuckles so sore cracked and numb

They favor a knot of bleeding wood.

If I look down (and I do look down) I see

That blood has poured from my back; seeped

Along the smoothness of my backside. Slid under

My testicles and coiled its way seductively

Around my thighs, knees and ebonised legs

It pours in abundance from my feet and skydives

I watch these red tears fall for ever and transform

Into explicit flowers as they reach the floor

I will not become one. I am hanging on.

I am hanging on. I am hanging on.

Whispers from above me. From above me whispers gather

The cliff ledge lined with edgy people of all colours

Some humming "Amazing grace" others simply staring

Some I saw pointing at my back and wincing.

A bearded man with his hand on a bible or a red book or
a white book

Or a leather book or a revolutionary book or a dark green
book

Shouted down to me in Sermonic tones deeper than the sea

"Let Go. In the name of God. Let Go!"

A nervous follower peeps down and offers the advice that

"There's someone down there, they'll catch you"

And before I get a chance to answer they erupt into a sky
shattering

"Someone's Crying Lord—Let Go. Someone's Crying
Lord—Let Go"

The harmony of those collected voices woke the spirit of
the sky

And they threw crosses at me. It's raining crosses.

I look down past my feet—a devil or a god

A man the size of a pea mouthing the words "Let Go"

Night-time was approaching. Breathless I whispered.

I will not fall. Never have. Never will. Not fall. Not fall.

But as quick as they came to help is as quick as they were
gone.

But I'm hanging on. I'm hanging on. I'm hanging on.

Darkness cloaked the horror of night-time

Of dangerous spirits that fed upon open wounds.

As lightning struck I saw glimpses of their faces;

Demons whose countenance had slipped;

Whose fingers had stretched and nails had curled

Whose breath stank so viciously that I spewed to the sea

(My mantra I am hanging on I am hanging on I am
     hanging on)

Throughout the darkness and fear until sunrise. And the
     stillness of

Mourning breaking. I was a silhouette hanging from a
     branch

Against the chalky cliff. Only the sound of my trickling
     blood,

My breaking back and the moaning sky for comfort.

My shadow stretching across the cliff like a script title

On handmade paper.

The sulking storm retreated into the horizon to recollect—

Even the sea is trying to throw off its reflection.

I listened more, to the tearing of my backflesh as I hang

The flapping wet skin of my bloodied back as it hangs

Tears painted salt veins along my ebonized skin.

As that stark sunlight skidded across a bloodied sky

I sensed the presence of two symmetrical shadows de-
     scending.

They stretched seemingly even pushing back the clouds

I felt them push warm air into my face.

I saw them in the corner of each of my eyes. Magnificent
     wings

And felt the new muscles on my back and my chest expand
     with air.

Further and further. New air. New Spirit. And there was
     not a soul around me

I unpeeled my tender fingers from that dew-drenched
   branch
I let the sun pour into my eyes and finally after years I
   let go. Why?
Because I was growing. I was growing wings all the time.
   And I can fly.

When he finished, my chest lifted. All my life I had been told to let go of my father, to say goodbye and move on. Here, I was invited to let go of the weight I bore to survive, in order to see the strength I had been building all along. In doing so, perhaps I too could be free of the burden forced upon me. This poet had given me what I so desperately needed to hear.

She sits in her counsellor's office, relaying her experience of the crime. The counsellor asks, "Didn't the nurses say they recognized him? That must mean he came knowingly to your house?"

Feeling confused, she shifts her eyes toward the window beside the counsellor and settles her gaze on the trees that run alongside the creek a few storeys below. This is the first time she's heard this information. *Why don't I know this already? Does everyone know about the case but me?* Questions rush through her mind. *Why is she telling me this here?* She notices the counsellor backtrack, likely realizing she had been repeating a rumour, one which no one had informed her of before.

Back home, she asks her mother, "Did Sheldon know him?"

"Oh, they couldn't prove it," she responds.

"What do you mean?"

"The police tried to prove it. That he came to our house on purpose. There were rumours of a guy at the hospital, cleaning staff or something, in a drug ring who found addresses for other hospital staff. Some other prisoners were saying things like that."

A stunned look appears on her face. She's just hearing this information, six years after the crime, and she wonders, *What else have I not been told? Why do people keep things secret?* She doesn't understand why it is her job to formulate the right questions, the correct sequence of words, in order to be given accurate information.

A rotting in her gut firmly takes hold. *What happened to my family?*

NO UNJUST
ACT UNNOTICED

Over two months after my visit with Sheldon in prison, I was sitting in a busy coffee shop marking students' papers when an email arrived on my phone. It was from Jennifer.

> I met with Sheldon earlier this month and have two updates
> for you. Would you like to have a quick conversation on the
> phone? Or if you prefer I can email you. Let me know.

Email is great, I answered, and said it was probably *for psychological reasons* that I hadn't sent a letter. I waited a few minutes for her reply.

Whenever it feels right, you can pass it along, she wrote, allaying my worries that she and Dave were judging my delayed response.

> In terms of my meeting with Sheldon, he wanted you to know
> that he did not find the Reasons for Judgment in any of his
> papers. I too have been unable to find them as of yet.

Hmmm, I thought. *How come?*

The other thing that Sheldon said had been on his mind was a concern that he may not have actually told you in person that he is sorry for taking your Dad's life. If that is the case, he is regretful of that.

Whoa, where did that come from? I placed my phone back on the table and pushed it aside. That word.

Sorry.

I'd never sought that word, never even really considered it. *What does that even mean?* I thought to myself. I was confused.

Two months later, I was sitting in a circle with twenty practicum students enrolled in the bachelor's degree program in child and youth care at the college. They had been placed at various social-services agencies around the Lower Mainland—schools, group homes, recreation centres.

"Okay, everyone, today we're going to talk about what's challenging you in your practicum placements," I said. "You've been there for a while now, so you've likely noticed things that bother you, things that you've struggled with, things that perhaps you don't understand or don't know how to handle." I looked around me and saw lots of nodding heads. "Let's go around the circle, and when someone offers an idea, feel free to comment."

The students began sharing examples of encounters in the field that reflected wider systemic problems: lack of funding, low standards in programming, practitioner competence, siloed disciplines, working from a place informed by fear, and lack of evidence-based practice. They, of course, did not name these scenarios in this way, but they'd soon learn. Instead, they described what they'd witnessed that caused them discomfort, and I understood it was my job to teach them to learn from that discomfort.

"I was in the staff lunch room the other day, and I didn't like what a teacher was saying," one student said. "He called a student an offensive word."

"Would you mind sharing it so we can understand?" I asked.

"He called him 'porcelain,'" she said.

"Where do you think that came from?"

"It's a boy who's being bullied by some other boys. I don't know him very well, but the teacher kept using that word."

The other students whispered to one another. "Does anyone have any immediate reflections on this situation?" I asked.

"The teachers at my school do that too, in the staff room," a student said.

"I wonder if we could avoid critiquing the teaching profession. Instead, let's focus on what's happening here. Let's focus first on the word 'porcelain.' What could that teacher mean by this word?"

"Breakable," one student offered.

"Weak," another said.

"Yes, a word like that conveys exactly those meanings. Now, let's take that one step further. If I were a person who thought that a boy was being weak in a bullying situation, what does that mean about how I think boys should behave?"

"They should be strong," a student said.

"And what does strong look like?" I said.

"Stand up to the bullies."

"Not break down."

"Yes, and those behaviours convey a particular way that a person thinks boys should behave," I said. "Now, we don't come up with ideas on our own. We're influenced by the people, ideas, and culture around us." We continued discussing how gender norms were often unhelpful and resulted in comments like these.

"Let's go back to this teacher. Do you think he cares about this student?"

"No," one student said.

"Really?" I challenged.

"Yes, I think he cares," another student said.

"I agree," I said. "But I also think that his approach could change. That he could foster strength in different ways. We're asking you to look at every situation like this. Think: What is happening that is invisible? What are the implicit factors that are influencing the situation?"

I returned home that night with a newfound confidence in my professional life. I knew that the social services system needed to change, and it first needed to change through language and a more nuanced understanding of what is harmful to young people. That night, I finally grasped the wisdom of my younger self, what she was already doing: calling attention to what was unjust, making my voice known. I'd become a child and youth worker to have more flexibility to support vulnerable people. Then I'd become a practice analyst to observe how the Ministry of Children and Family Development was and was not providing ethical and effective care. Now I was a teacher in a classroom, asking a new generation of learners to do the same. *What if I could offer what I instinctively knew how to do when I was young*: to make sure no unjust act went unnoticed, that no voice went unheard.

In a fury, she walks briskly toward her bedroom. Her mother follows, fuming. They are in the middle of an argument. Her sisters study quietly in their rooms, doors closed, and her brother watches television downstairs. These days, the yelling never seems to stop.

"What am I supposed to do?" her mother screams, lost and not knowing what her daughter needs nor why she has chosen tonight to let things boil over.

The girl's body is hot, her fingers are stretched apart, her hands up in the air. She tries to formulate words, yelling down the hallway back at her mother, "Why do you care for them, and you never care for me?"

"Because," her mother answers, desperately. "You," she says clearly, "can take care of yourself."

The girl slams her bedroom door and sits down against it, curling her body into itself. She puts her feet up flat on the wall, palms braced on the floor, and pushes as hard as she can in all directions.

She screams. Her voice is as loud as she can make it. Her mouth is wide open.

ONE HUNDRED AND THIRTY-EIGHT DAYS

It took one hundred and thirty-eight days after I met Sheldon to say what I needed to say.

Buoyed by my confidence and new insights after the session wth the practicum students, I wrote to him that night, sitting on the couch, lights dimmed, in the comfort and safety that I had constructed, in the world that I had worked so hard to create.

January 28, 2013

Sheldon,

Well, I'm writing this much beyond the timeline that I expected to. As I processed the meeting we had in September, the weeks went by, then months. And now, here I am writing to you in January 2013. It wasn't that I was overwhelmed by anything that was said between us. I had some things to say that took some time for me to realize how to say them.

Midway through our conversation in the morning, you told me a story of your life in June 1992. How after a series of decisions on one particular night, you ended up in the hospital. You came back to the hospital to be evaluated after killing my dad. And the nurses informed you that while you were being operated on, my dad—the orthopedic surgeon resident at Foothills—was your surgeon. You said the nurses told you that my dad told the police to leave you alone, that he wouldn't let them get your blood to confirm your blood-alcohol levels were over the limit. From what you said, this information surprised you, when the nurses told you who he was after you killed him. Then, in our conversation, you went back to June 1992 again. At that point you said that you remembered my dad. You described his physical appearance, his demeanor, and his personality as he treated you after your significant pelvic injury. You said that he joked with you, that you were 'on your own' when you decided to leave the hospital against physician's recommendations.

It is this piece of our meeting that I wish to reflect on and there are two parts.

First of all, I was so unbelievably satisfied to hear this information. What this knowledge meant to me was that you had experienced my father's presence. You had a glimpse of who he was—and the way you described him, his physicality, his personality, his way of being was exactly how I knew him to be and who exists in my mind. He was silly, caring, joyful, matter-of-fact, loving, real, and cared deeply for whomever sat across from him, even if they turned out to be the person who would 3 months later kill him. To me, what this means is that you know who you took away. No victim impact statement, no courtroom proceedings, no letter from me, no conversation, could convey to you who he was as a human being. Now I know that you know.

The second piece is a bit more complicated. It is my understanding that 20 years ago, police could not prove definitively that you knew my dad and that you came to my house purposefully. And so the topic stayed uncertain. I cannot tell you how disturbing this is, as a child and now adult; it is the uncertainty that is disturbing. Close to the beginning of this letter exchange process, I told you I had heard rumours that you knew my dad somehow. You said that you did not, but you'd been informed that you had been in the hospital and that my dad may have been working on your case somehow, but that you were unconscious the entire time. I accepted this information. Then, when we met in September, you told me that the nurses told you my dad performed surgery on you when you were severely injured and that he was instrumental in the police not criminalizing your criminal behaviour. Then, you went back to that encounter and shared that you in fact did remember my dad. You remember him being different than the other physicians. You remember his personality, caring for you and treating you like a human being. You, at this meeting, maintained that you did not come to my house on purpose, to kill my father.

It is this sequence of events—not the content but the process—that causes me concern. It seems immensely implausible that you randomly selected our garage to break into and steal tools or perhaps my dad's car. Statistically, considering your encounter with him in the hospital in June, it is actually quite probable that you came to my house on purpose. There could be many ways you figured this out and there could be many reasons why you wanted to locate my particular house. But let's leave statistics alone, because only you know the truth, the entire truth. That is the absolute power that you hold. You can see how I could come to the conclusion that you are slowly telling me the truth and that I can expect to be told the entire truth in due time. Or perhaps you think you've told enough of the truth, somehow justifying to yourself that telling bits and pieces is just.

Let me tell you the story I've constructed in my head: I think you were curious about my dad. Perhaps you thought he was an interesting man, much different than the people who you've come across in your life, particularly the people who have been in caring roles. Perhaps you saw him get into his car in the hospital parking lot. Perhaps you followed him home. Perhaps you took a look in the phone book for his name and saw my address. Perhaps you were stoned out of your mind and found out where he lived and just went to visit—perhaps you can't even remember the entire story but know pieces. You've had 20 years of forced reflection to recall. I really don't know. But perhaps you saw an opportunity three months previous to you seeing an opportunity with an open window in my house. Perhaps you wanted to see how he lived, what he was like, or perhaps it was just that you wanted to steal his car. Again, I really don't know, and I'll never know until you tell me.

All I know is that you've slowly shared information, implicitly or explicitly claiming that the information that you've just shared is the entire truth of the situation. But then you share more. You can surely understand my distrust.

This conflict in information is what has caused me most concern, upset, and angst over the past 5 months. And I couldn't write to you to communicate this 4 months ago. And then I realized why—

This information is your responsibility to share. With

me. It is not my responsibility to ask the right questions; it's not even my responsibility to ask in the first place. This is your responsibility as a human being. You hold the power of knowing what happened. And keeping that information to yourself—during the investigation, during the trial, during the appeals, during your 20 years of life in prison thus far—is part of what you're responsible for. You're not just responsible for the death, but the lies. Because what makes death worse—and whomever thought that there could be something worse than a person violently murdered in their home with their family surrounding them—are the lies, the uncertainty felt by all people but you. It's your responsibility to be completely forthcoming, without any self-interest.

Now, you could be withholding this information for fear of known or unknown ramifications. Perhaps one of those reasons is that I will get mad/upset—and you don't want me to experience more pain. More likely, one of those possible reasons is because of any future applications, hearings, etc. regarding your parole. These are all possibilities. And I don't care about any of them. I care about knowing what happened to me. And you hold not only the power to ruin my life 20 years ago but also to withhold information for me understanding what happened.

I'm going to leave that there for you to reflect on and decide what to do, because I've had enough of wondering.

Later in the fall, Jennifer sent me an email just checking in. She said that she met with you earlier in November and had an update to share.

One was that you couldn't find anything in your documents that is similar to my request—some kind of Reasons for Judgment. She said she could not find this either. You probably requested the documents from your lawyer. In order for me, however, to access court documents, I not only have to learn who to ask, I also have to be told that the best way to access them is through the person who killed my father. Do you think that's a bit ironic? I do. This is of course not your problem, but I thought I'd bring it to your attention because you mentioned that you had what seemed to be thousands of pieces of paper from your various court cases. I am just looking for a judge's words, which includes his decision and why he gave you the sentence he did. I have been told this happens at the end of a trial. You're familiar with these documents, I will assume, so I'd appreciate if you could look again.

The other thing that Jennifer included in your message to me was that you're sorry for killing my father and that you regret not having told me this in person.

Unless you're sorry for each and every thing you did wrong, then being sorry for killing my father becomes a bit meaningless. Don't you think?

Are you sorry for the drugs you took before you began your evening adventure to my neighbourhood?

Are you sorry for all of the other garages you broke into?

Are you sorry for the family's of those garages, who you scared, having their safety violated in that particular way?

Are you sorry for not taking my father's directives to stay longer in the hospital while you were clearly still recovering from being injured months before you came to my house?

Are you sorry for not asking for any help that would have been provided to you for your dependency on drugs?

Are you sorry for approaching my house?

Are you sorry for looking in the windows where my siblings were sleeping?

Are you sorry for touching my house's door handle?

Are you sorry for opening my house's door?

Are you sorry for stepping into my house?

Are you sorry for looking at my father's jackets in the closet?

Are you sorry for picking up a knife?

Are you sorry you were so selfish that you were defending yourself with that knife?

Are you sorry that you didn't run when you heard my dad's voice?

Are you sorry you didn't run after?

Are you sorry that you actively slammed a knife into my dad's body, not once but three times, the same man who took a knife to your body in surgery to save it?

Are you sorry you didn't call the police immediately to turn yourself in?

Are you sorry you spent hours at your brother's home waiting?

Are you sorry for not taking your first lawyers' advice?

Are you sorry for lying to lawyers, police, judges, jurors? Not just once, but moments upon moments, for years upon years.

Are you sorry for lying to my family?

Are you sorry for lying and withholding information from me?

Are you sorry for the energy, money, and time it took for your appeals to go through, all while knowing you were lying, wasting society's finances and my family's psychological well-being, both wondering—is it the right guy?

Are you sorry for the thousands of moments I've lost with my father and he's lost with me?

Are you sorry for the pain you caused for the thousands of people my dad connected with in his lifetime?

Have you apologized to my father?

The flipside of sorry, I hear, is forgiveness. I hear many people's definitions of the word, none of which I'm sold on. I hear forgiveness is more about the person who's been hurt—the 'victim'—so that they can move on, whatever that means. Some people, some religions think that an apology and forgiveness is an absolute must. I haven't been schooled in religious practices, the ones that are drilled into children's minds through stories of life's meaning, justice according to God, and also shame and guilt. I wonder if the apology/forgiveness process simplifies things, let's everyone involved blindly move forward. But this could just be my ignorance of the significant history of this process. Nonetheless, this is where I am. I mean, I'm an advocate for the Canadian Government's apology to the Indigenous peoples of Canada, but not because they're sorry. Being sorry is so selfish—puts the focus on the person who's done the harm. Rather, I'm more interested in hearing the Government say that they did something wrong—atrocious wrongs—that obliterated a people. And then I'm interested in seeing them do everything in their power to make things right. Action being the key piece.

So what if forgiveness has nothing to do with anything. What if it's not a necessary part?

To me, an apology means nothing. Just more selfish words, coming after a selfish series of acts—from the moment you even thought of entering my home to the last appeal court you applied to. Apologies are just words until they are actions. So I'm not so much interested in hearing your apology, giving you forgiveness, and then coming to some mutual satisfaction with regard to the wrong you brought into my world. By all of this I'm not implying that I think what you're currently doing in your day-to-day life is not okay—in fact, I think quite the opposite. I am looking for you to contribute something to someone else's life, not take away from it. I'm looking for you to do good work that doesn't hurt people. Statistically, there's very little chance that you're going to commit murder again. But if we all held that low standard of expectation for ourselves—that we get through life without murdering someone (again)—that's a pretty pathetic existence. I have the highest expectations of myself and others. This gets me into trouble, as you can imagine—mostly with the expectations I hold of myself. However, it is also my ultimate strength—I see potential in people, of what they can do. Integrity is the most important thing in the world to me.

So here's what I'm sorry for. I'm sorry that our collective society leaves people to survive day to day, ripening the ground for people to select breaking into homes instead of building homes, or stealing parts from a work yard instead of creating parts that help the world move forward. I'm sorry that we deal with drugs through our corrections system, not our health and social care systems. I'm sorry that right now there exists young people with similar life histories as yours, sitting in youth detention or on probation or searching for drugs to numb their lives or provide them a daily living; and I'm sorry that some of those young people will continue to have stories like yours—having the opportunity to change course only after they've destroyed something. I'm sorry that people's lives lead them to not care about themselves and others. And I'm sorry that we collectively agree that crime & punishment has anything to do with paying your debt to society.

Most of all, I'm sorry that you never had the opportunity to experience a father like mine, a flawed human being with a caring, creative, life-giving, and passionate soul. But I'm not saying sorry and then going on to do nothing about it. The work I contribute to the world has integrity, and I remind myself of that expectation every day, because I'll be damned if I have lived my life contributing to destruction.

So please don't be sorry. If you need to say this to yourself, then that's just fine, that's your process. You don't owe me an apology. What you owe me is to say what you did wrong—all of it. And I've sincerely appreciated what you've told me thus far; it has changed my life. What you owe me is to make things right. Make it right. That's your responsibility. And it's mine too.

I look forward to your response,

Carys

I finished writing, attached the letter in an email to Dave and Jennifer, and closed my computer. I leaned back on my couch, a weight lifted off me. No one could have told me how good it would feel to write it. To write what was wrong.

She leaves home. She stays with a friend who she knows won't judge her, although others do.

"You should go home. You're making your family upset," some of her close friends tell her. She wonders why they're not curious as to why she left in the first place. She looks at them and judges them right back for not understanding.

While she stays with her friend, they spend their evenings and weekends playing Spy vs. Spy, a game where they drive through the city with a water gun, trying to capture classmates on a list. They attend a school dance, and she sneaks out of the house while her friend is at soccer practice to kiss a boy on the beach. She even gets her homework done: a map for her geography class, trigonometry calculations for her mathematics class, and a series of photographs for her photography class that she'll develop in the lab. She writes an in-class essay for social studies, where her ideas flow easily, a new experience. She takes time to write in her journal.

I've been at my friend's place for a week now. So many things have happened. I haven't cried since Friday afternoon so I'm proud of that. I left for many reasons. Some having to do with mom and the rest, me. Many people have said that it's unfair of me to put my family in this situation. Well, I probably should go home but sometimes life isn't the way it should be. For instance, I should have a father but I don't. I am being selfish but I think it is for a good cause. I'm leaving home cause I would like to be happy.

Something has to change in our family before I go back.

I have an idea of what but it doesn't seem possible. I'm a good daughter. I clean. I do my homework. I study. I get straight A's. I don't get wasted every weekend. I don't drive recklessly. Why does everyone take advantage of the fact that I'm strong and I won't get mad at them. I don't want to be controlled by them. It has to stop.

After two weeks, she feels uncomfortable, like she is imposing, and asks her mother's best friend if she can stay in her unoccupied basement suite.

"Your mother would like you to be at home," she is told. "You can't stay here. You two will work it out."

She feels embarrassed for asking and at a loss about what to do.

Resigned, she returns home and wonders why she felt freer in those two weeks than she'd ever felt. Her mother promises that things will change, that she'll listen, that they'll stop fighting, but they don't. They don't change.

She learns her lesson: sometimes people say what they need to in the moment. They say, or do not say, what meets their own needs, not necessarily the needs of the person they are responsible for.

NEVER ENOUGH

26

don't know. I wasn't thinking," Mom said when I challenged her on why she supposed I could give the letters to my brother so he could go meet Sheldon.

"Exactly," I said, staring across the restaurant table over brunch.

"I just thought—I always think you're brave. You were doing what you were doing. You've always done that, and I admire that."

"It didn't feel that way," I told her.

"You're always ahead of the game," she said.

"But I feel so alone. And when you do those things, it feels like you're taking advantage of me."

"That's not what I intend," she said. "Keep doing what you're doing."

With that, I understood. The only way she knew to support me was to just let me go do it. Mom had confidence in me. She focused her attention elsewhere, where she felt more effective.

"I regret two things," she said with a mournful expression. "I regret moving away from Calgary. We had a life there. I could have taken a job there."

I continually tried to process the decisions Mom made at and after the time of Dad's death and was constantly reminding myself that she made them out of sheer survival. In a split second her wonderful life was ruined. Left on her own with four children to raise, she moved us back to Vancouver to find a new job, a new house, a new life. But Calgary was our home.

"I get it, Mom. Your parents were here, your sisters, your best friends. Grandma and Grandpa were like second parents."

"I regret it, though," she said. "All of you—we had a life there."

Tears built up in my eyes. It was healing to hear these words. It meant there could have been another life—a life where people we knew cared for us, where I wouldn't have to explain myself, where familiarity comforted our souls while we healed. That life, it was clear, didn't exist. But it could have, and I took comfort in knowing that the losses I had experienced and the challenges I'd had adapting—all while dealing with a murdered father—were valid. They were additional losses that didn't help an already traumatic situation.

"What was the second thing?" I asked.

"I regret not realizing how smart you four were."

"What do you mean?"

"I now know that kids process what's happening and want information. I didn't realize that you were aware of what was happening and wanted to know things. If I'd known that, I would have told you everything. You were seeking it out anyhow."

I looked at her, regretting, too, what she hadn't known, the injustice to her. She was a parent just trying to do her best, and it could never have been enough.

The wind grew strong as I stepped out of my car a block away from the CJI offices. I looked up into the bright, clear sky, heard the rustling of the late spring leaves.

Knowing the drill, I walked into the offices, greeted the familiar faces, and was accompanied to the small boardroom. Normally, it took two weeks at most for Sheldon to reply to my letters. He had finally responded to my most recent, and most challenging, letter, after close to three months. They passed his letter to me and, with it, what looked like a court transcript. I began to read.

April 22, 2013

Dear Carys,

Wow where to begin! First things first, I have been honest with you about every single aspect of our conversations. So with that I will try to explain to you what was on my mind while I was in the hospital and what took place before I met your father, which was only for a very brief moment. The only thing was on my mind was tending to my wounds and getting home. I know that I had been a very lucky individual that night; knowing I was the only one that was severely injured came as a relief to me. The implication of me sitting at a window watching for your father as he gets into his car is not only dumbfounding but absurd. Wondering if I can break into his home 3 months later seems to be a very patient and methodical thing to do, even borderline psychotic. This and the mindset I was in at the time of the accident just do not come hand in hand. Before the accident I was getting hooked on drugs and trying to feed the animal inside of me. I did not leave the hospital with the intent to get hooked on drugs. This is what happened to have been in front of me at the time. I never said to anyone that I would like to break into garages. This is what someone had said to me. I went along with this because I really didn't have other options financially my life was in turmoil as was my ability to make good decisions.

I had been out at a club with my roommate after a night of indulgence of something that was given to me by a so called friend. I had one Coors light and went home. I was sitting there wondering if I should go out. I decided to take a car that I had stolen a day earlier. The part of town I was living in had nothing for me. So I decided to drive. I ended up in your part of town. And the rest is history. There was no thought there was no conspiracy, this was pure coincidence. I swear on my life that this chance meeting was what it is and nothing more. I have no motive to not tell you the truth I told you that I met your father I did. I found out that your dad had worked on me at the hospital emergency room. There was no surgery. I was unconscious or slipping in and out of it. The next day or so a doctor had come into my room to check on his patient. I remember asking when I can leave and he said that I should stay a couple of days. When he left, one of my friends told me that the police were there to take my blood and they were denied. I don't know how he got this info but that was reiterated to me.

The next time I saw your dad I was ready to go home. He told me to sign some papers and that I should take it easy. He kind of explained to me about what I need to do to take care of myself and that I might feel this injury once I'm old and grey. I would like to point out one other scenario here.

I don't want this to sound to confusing but I need you to understand that this is what it is, nothing more. If I hadn't gone to this hospital I would never of known this information, thus neither would you. This information is not my salvation here I'm already pretty much done the max sentence here. There is nothing anybody can do to me. I told you from the beginning of this journey that I was going to be honest with you. I didn't have to tell you that I had met your father. You asked me if I had known your father. You asked me if I had known your father. I do not know him. I know of him and tried really hard to remember him most in part for your sake. It seemed really important to you that we had met and had a conversation. This was important to me. I wanted to connect with you and let you know that I do understand the pain I have caused through out my life.

I would like you to know that twenty years have gone by and I will always be the man that killed your father. I will always be the man that lied about it. I will always be the man that tried to blame an innocent man for my miss deed. I will always be the man that will never live up to people's expectation. I will always be the boy that was abused. I will always be the boy that no one will trust or wanted. I will always be the man that has learned from his past mistakes and will try and strive to be a better person. I have been the man that has been telling you the truth. The person I was is no longer the person I am.

If you can't accept that then we have reached an impasse here. I want you to know that I was a little disappointed that you think I'm being shady with you. I do believe your questioning does have merit and like I said before I will always tell you the truth. I have held nothing back despite my past lies.

I want you to know that I will look into getting you the information you requested. If you choose to continue to write to me I will read your letters and respond to what you say in those letters. I enjoy speaking with you about anything you want to talk about although I kind of feel raked over the coals with your last letter. But feel that you deserve to know the truth about everything. I hope I have cleared things up for you, So please feel free to write back if you so desire. If this is where it ends then goodbye and good luck with everything that you want to accomplish in your life.

Sheldon

I lifted my head and saw Susan and Dave's empathetic faces staring back at me, waiting for me to finish reading.

I shook my head in disappointment. *God forbid I call his attention to his inconsistencies*, I thought.

"I think he's reached his capacity to respond. I don't think he understands what I'm asking of him," I said.

Dave and Susan were listening to me calmly.

"He thinks I'm making up some story about him knowing my dad," I continued. "And there's one sentence I really don't like—'I didn't have to tell you.'" *Have to*, as though he was being altruistic when, in fact, this was about being truthful. *If it happened, say it. If it didn't, don't say it. But don't do something just for me,* I thought.

"I do think he's mimicking my phrasing, the repetition of 'I will always be that guy.' I appreciate that. I really do."

"Do you think it's genuine?" Dave asked.

"Yes, I think it's as genuine as can be. I think he's being as responsive as he can possibly be." I thought that was an honest answer—and ultimately it wasn't going to be enough. It would never be enough, given his incapacity to tell the truth.

"Yes, I do too," Dave said.

"I think it's over."

"You don't have to know right now," Dave said.

"You know, it's the funniest thing. When you and Sandi said that I'd send the letters through you, and then they'd go through Jennifer in Alberta before they'd reach Sheldon, I was curious to know what it would be like for people I didn't know to read my words, the most intimate and intense thoughts. A few of my friends were taken aback, almost like someone reading your journal, and they wondered how that might be disruptive. But that's not the case." I paused.

"I can't tell you how lovely it's been to have you all read my words, to know that they're protected and carried to him, and to know that his are as well, on their way to me. In a situation where safety is everything, thank you for being our words' protectors. Thank you so much."

"It's our privilege," Susan said.

Her history teacher assigns her a research paper on what she later learns is called the Great Man Theory. She puzzles over the paper's implicit question: Do great men create events that mold history or is it the events that create great men?

She approaches her teacher after school.

"But how could it be either/or?" she asks.

"Exactly," he says in return. "Now go write that."

She drives across town, uses her older cousin's student library card to sit in the university library's basement stacks, and reads about the infinite factors that influenced political leaders centuries ago. She'll always remember the dilemma she takes away: Are people a product of their environment or do they have the ability to change their surroundings, big and small?

She doesn't care about the grade, but she will always remember how her teacher shakes her hand in front of the class.

Her teachers care for her and mentor her, when her family cannot.

REASONS
FOR JUDGMENT

Dave and Susan were silent as I shuffled through the stack of papers. "So he found the Reasons for Judgment section of the trial transcripts? Is that what this is, in the file?" I asked them. *Funny*, I thought, *that he found it at my demand, after telling me he couldn't.*

There were twenty-one typed pages, each line of the transcript numbered along the left side of the page. I began to read.

> In the court of Queen's Bench of Alberta, Judicial District of
>   Calgary
> Her Majesty the Queen v Sheldon Thane Klatt, Accused
> Sentencing
> Calgary, Alberta, 16th July, 1993

I turned the page and found the salient words first spoken by the Crown prosecutor.

> Section 744 sets out the matters that should be considered by the
> court in making a determination as to whether or not a period
> of parole and eligibility should be increased upwards from ten

years anywhere to 25. And they set out that the criteria is the age and character of the accused, the nature of the offence and the circumstances surrounding it, and the recommendation of the jury.

I skimmed the lines.

Now I would like to review those principles and criteria.

First of all, the character of the accused. The accused has a lengthy criminal record ... It appears since the age of 15 he has been convicted of a serious crime including some charges of escaping lawful custody.

In addition to his record, I submit you can and should take into consideration the disreputable conduct that the accused testified to himself when he was on the stand under oath. And that included, truthful or otherwise, he said he committed some 50 garage break-ins, two house break-ins and that he deals in the sale of cocaine. All of these offences, I understood him to say, occurred last summer.

Secondly, in dealing with his character, I ask the court to consider that the accused testified and that a jury having made the finding that they have—must have made a finding that the accused fabricated evidence. The accused lied and that the accused committed perjury ...

Thirdly, I ask the court to consider that in not only testifying but in voluntary statements given to the police on a number of occasions, the accused accused an innocent person of the crime that he committed. That crime itself being the most heinous crime of murder ...

Those matters, I submit, show that he is indeed a most manipulative person and that he has absolutely no remorse whatsoever for this terrible crime that he has committed.

Fifthly, in regard to the character of the accused, I ask you to consider a psychiatric assessment done while in the forensic unit. Done for the court and submitted to the court on the basis of whether he was fit to stand trial ...

I scanned the findings of the assessment.

... knows the nature of the charges and the consequences ...

does not suffer from mental illness of a psychotic kind, nor is he depressed ...

long history of anti-social behaviour, willingly rejecting society's rules leading to a diagnosis of anti-social personality disorder ...

diagnosis of alcohol and cocaine abuse ...

he was cooperative but unpleasant ...

he was continually watchful and not forthcoming in information requested ...

while on the unit, Mr. Klatt was manipulative, at times angry and uncooperative, always watchful of the staffs' movements ...

there were frequent contradictions in what he told us compared to the collateral information available to us ...

there is some psycho-social assessment in regard to his father being physically abusive and an alcoholic ...

states that he lied, stole, ran away from home frequently as a child until made ward of the court at age 11 ...

Age eleven.

... subsequently increased his delinquency to fire settings, destruction of public property, assault, assault of a peace officer and break and enter ...

at the age of 18 he is charged with auto theft and convicted of break and enter and convicted of a trafficking in firearms offence ...

They could have stopped him, I thought.

... cognitive testing revealed no evidence of memory impairment or confusion ...

the court should be concerned about granting bail while incarcerated ...

treatments for the types of personality difficulties that affect him have proven to be of little value ...

The second matter that should be taken into consideration is the nature of the offence ... Killing a person in their own home. A vicious forceful stabbing. So forceful and so vicious it caused the knife to shatter into four pieces. The accused armed himself as he broke into this person's home. I submit that a person's home is his last refuge and every person should be allowed to feel safe in his own home. The victim had to protect his wife and his four young children. This crime was done in their presence and I suggest and submit the nature of the offence has been and is an outrage in this community ...

The crime has caught the attention of the entire community. The community should be able to feel safe in their own homes. For a person to steal into the sanctity of that home in the middle of the night, arm themselves and kill the resident when confronted, I submit to you has left this community in fear that it could happen to them ...

I skimmed over the references to other cases and continued reading.

> The jury has made a recommendation in the strongest terms
> that they can of 25 years. It is the highest recommendation they
> could possibly make. I submit that society has spoken and the
> community has spoken through this jury ... They heard the
> evidence. They made the finding of fact. They didn't have to
> make that recommendation but they did. And because it was so
> emphatic, it cannot and should not be ignored. The jury, I submit,
> speaks for the community ... Society needs to be protected from
> this person.

Next, I read the defense counsel's remarks:

> My client testified but he had made admissions which saved,
> in my respectful submission, any further trauma to the family
> ... There is some background in his record, that is an extensive
> record, there is not much violence.

After reading the first sentences, I could see he was going to try
to minimize the gravity of the crime, so I skimmed ahead.

> The clear danger, in my respectful submission, is that the com-
> munity through this court allow its repugnance to overwhelm it,
> overwhelm its reason and its need for justice ... To listen solely to
> a need for retribution is an error and it is not just.

And then, finally, after twenty years of wondering what the judge
concluded, I read his words: *Stand up, Mr. Klatt. Anything you wish
to say before I pass sentence on you?*

Sheldon responded, *This is a tragedy and I believe that there is a man out there that has ruined two lives, not just one. And I hope the courts will administer justice with sympathy.*

The judge instructed him to sit and began his sentencing.

> With respect to those comments, I can only say that a jury of 12 impartial citizens heard the evidence and decided that there was not another man out there who has ruined two lives. And I fully agree with them. I would have taken much less time to come to the same conclusion than they did.
>
> I think that Mr. Klatt's statement is the only indication I need of the character of the man to guide me in sentencing. The reference to ruining two lives shows the shallowness of the individual. Concerned about himself and, of course, the obvious victim ... Read the victim impact statements, Mr. Klatt. It affects a lot of people. It ruins a lot of lives.
>
> I am not going to take a lot of time. I agree absolutely with everything the Crown says. There is no element of retribution in the sentence I am going to impose. I do this not to be vengeful ... I do not detect in the victim impact statements any element of retribution or vengeance. They are a graceful, eloquent expression of the effect of this crime on many, many innocent people ...
>
> I believe the evidence of the witnesses. I believe the evidence of the other occupants of the Remand Centre, at least the last one, who says a couple of days before the trial started, the statements were being passed around by Klatt. For what purpose, to intimidate them.
>
> In addition to the hoax attempted on the system, Klatt also is prone to using threats of violence to others. That is a serious aggravating factor in this case.

Further, the idea that this was just another break-in, who's going to care about it, the police aren't going to chase me, I can give my name to a cab driver, no big deal. The break-in of a residence is a big deal. The people of Canada have said that the penalty for breaking into a residence is life imprisonment. That is the most serious penalty that the law can impose. The question of parole and eligibility are not the same form of matter. The sentence is life imprisonment for murder, the sentence for the break-and-enter of a residence can be life imprisonment as well. It is a big deal. The person who has the attitude that the break-and-enter of a private residence is no big deal, is a threat to every occupant of dwellings in this city.

Another aspect of this case which is perhaps somewhat unusual is we heard not only from the accused as to the attitude he has to break-ins, but we have heard from people who obviously, in my view, have similar attitudes. The last three witnesses for the defense. All from the Remand Centre. All young individuals. All with records going back to their pre-adult days. I am sure they share the same attitude as Klatt does to break-ins. No big deal. The time has come to let these young people who start their life of crime, in some cases even before their teenage years, know that break-ins are a big deal. You take it too far, the law will go the limit.

And then he said it.

Stand up.
You are sentenced to life imprisonment. No parole for 25 years.

I finished the report, laid it down on top of Sheldon's letter, and began to cry, holding my body tight.

"I'm okay," I said, preempting a comment from Dave or Susan. I didn't want them to worry about me. Surely they'd seen the spectrum of their clients' emotions, more in one year than most people witness in a lifetime. But I couldn't stop the tears. "I promise I'm okay," I assured them again. I didn't want them thinking that I was scared in response to what I had just read or that it had been a bad idea to read the transcript in the first place.

"These tears, they're just ... they're not about this," I faltered.

"They're just ... I just ..."

I held my body tighter.

"I just love my dad so much."

Sitting on a patio chair, she brings her knees up to her chest, the soles of her feet resting on the seat. The wind begins to pick up, so she wraps a blanket around herself.

She is not sure where the rest of her family is; that's not information they share with one another. Perhaps at sports practice, at work, or out with friends.

The sky is clear. She looks out at the islands that extend across the water. She will miss this view when she goes away to university in the fall. As the sun sets to the west, the glow of pinkish red spreads across the horizon. Noticing the eagles flying overhead, she watches them swoop down near the water and soar back up to their resting place in the towering trees nearby. Her breathing slows and becomes deeper, as if to take in every bit of fresh evening air.

Holding her journal on her knees with one hand and a pen with the other, she begins to write to her father.

I think that's all you need to know in life. How to have fun. Everything else just falls into place. Daddy, you knew how to have fun. At least you looked like you were having fun, and everyone else says you were the best at having fun. I want to be like you. But I can't, at least it's hard when you're gone. All I really have is memories and pictures and stories to look at for your guidance. And I know that's enough, but it's still very hard.

I really want to be purely happy. And I honestly think that by going away and doing everything for myself (not for mom, not for guys, not for girlfriends, not for anyone—maybe even not for you, daddy) then maybe I'll be happy. It's true, you have to make yourself happy first. Then you can be happy with other people. You have to love yourself. Then you can love someone else.

She stretches her neck and looks around.

But what comes first? Do you have to learn how to be happy before you can love yourself? Or is it that you have to love yourself to be happy? Either way—how do you love yourself or how do you become happy?

I think they're the same thing—don't you?

She puts her journal down beside her chair. Repositioning herself beneath the blanket, she watches darkness reach across the sky.

She thinks to herself, *Is that what he was trying to teach me?*

28
AT THE HELM

Unlike the previous letters, which took weeks or months to write, the words came quickly and easily out of my mouth as I drove home, and when I got there, I typed them immediately on my laptop.

April 27, 2013

Sheldon,

So here we are. This is the last letter I will write to you for the time being. I cannot predict whether I will want to write to you or see you again. Part of me wanted to speak my last letter's words to you in person so that we could have a conversation about those pieces. But I think what was said in person needed to be said in person and what was said in the letters needed to be said in the letters. It is what it is.

I could get into discussing my intentions with that letter. I can appreciate that you felt as though you've been 'raked over the coals,' but for me that wasn't what that was about nor will I feel bad for what I said. And I can appreciate that you've interpreted my questioning as though I've made some kind of story in my mind and that you think coming to my house on purpose would be absurd, but for me that wasn't what that was about.

Yes, you will always be that man who did all of those things.
Every single one of them.

I broke from writing. His letter focused on himself, how he thought it was absurd for me to think he came to my house on purpose. I thought of all the times I've wanted to curl up with my younger self and let her know that in twenty years she will feel free of the burden she has been forced to carry.

I was seeking something from him that I knew I would never get. It was ludicrous of me to even try, but I had to. It was not until that moment—the end of this process—that I discovered why I'd needed to do all this.

So I wrote it down for him.

> The intention of my last letter was to ask for empathy from you, to acknowledge that it seems plausible there could have been some reason why you came to my house. This isn't about arguing. This is about me having to live with that question in my mind, having people think and say this about my family, and you showing empathy that that is the unfair situation I must live with for the rest of my life.

I thought of my younger self, trying to survive the best I could. The thing I needed to hear would have to come from myself. This discovery shook me to my core.

> So maybe I should just show myself some empathy, realize that I have no control or responsibility in this case. It is what it is.

My body warmed, and I began to feel energy surging through

every cell. Tears of relief started streaming down my face. I had no idea how good it would feel, and that it was within me all along. I'd finally got what I needed. I was so wonderfully, completely, and finally done.

> Our worlds collided, and they have once more. And I have appreciated throughout this time that they've been on my terms. So, while I don't think we've reached an impasse, as you reflect, I do think we've reached an ending. I hope that we both get to lead long and wonderful lives so that anything is possible, that we can move past 5 year plans and 25 year prison sentences and move forward, past survival and into something so much more.
>
> All I know is this. My dad made everyone around him a better person. I feel so lucky to be his daughter, even if he was only right next to me for 11 years. Perhaps he'll do the same for you so that you can become more than the man who did all those horrible acts. Maybe his life has offered you something different. Now that I know you, this is what I wish for. Thank you for listening. Thank you for responding. Thank you for writing. And that, I believe, is my forgiveness.
>
> Carys

I pressed Send, and then it was over.

A few days later, I stared at the pile of letters in the file folder sitting on my desk. I wondered, *What am I going to do with these?* For two years I'd wanted to keep them close. But as soon as I sent the last letter, I felt a compelling desire to get rid of them all.

I scanned them into my computer and made a file deep in my digital archives. I then placed his letters and mine in sequential order and stuffed them into my bag. It was a beautiful day, and I knew where I needed to go.

I parked in the cul-de-sac at the end of the road that led to the public beach where I'd been so many times: to remember my father, to scatter his ashes, to celebrate my accomplishments, and to connect. I walked down the rocky path flanked by tall trees, stepping down the hill one solidly placed foot at a time. A few people sat along the beach's rocky shore. I wandered my way over the rocks to a private area on the west side of the bay's curve. Laying a beach towel on the rock just a few feet above the water and positioning myself, rather uncomfortably, behind a large boulder, I pulled the stack of letters out of my bag and began to tear up each page after I read it aloud. Page by page, I threw each tiny piece into the sea.

I recalled standing on the sailboat deck with my family, anchored in the same bay, passing along the bag of Dad's cremated ashes. When it was passed to me, I stretched my hands out as I poured the contents out of the bag, feeling him falling through my fingers, then into the sea. I breathed in the dust left on my fingers.

By the time I reached the last page of the last letter, hundreds of flecks of paper were swirling between the rocks below the water's surface, trapped in the current. They twirled round and round as the sea chewed them up and swallowed them.

I stood up and looked around at the bright late-afternoon sun. Walking precariously over the rocks, I passed some older women who were sunbathing and smiled at them. To the left of the bay's curve there was a child navigating the rocky ground, the mother close behind, watching over him. I reached the grass at the base of the hill and saw a young couple embracing, seated on one of my father's benches placed there twenty years earlier.

My father's plaque was attached to a rock next to the benches. I knelt and read the dedication, as I had many times before.

Dr. Geoffrey A. Cragg

I would rather be a superb meteor, every atom of me in
magnificent glow, than a sleepy permanent planet. The proper
function of a man is to live, not to exist. I shall not waste days
in trying to prolong them. I shall use my time.

—Jack London

Dedicated to the wonderful spirit of this man from his
many friends and loving family.

I kissed my fingers and placed them upon the rock, then stood up, and as I smiled at the couple, I walked away.

Soon after, sitting across from two colleagues, I interviewed for another teaching contract at the college, though it was more of a conversation than an interview.

"You should think about doing your PhD," one of them said.

"No kids, no mortgage," reasoned the other. "Now's the best time."

I felt complimented that they would recommend I undertake advanced study in our field. Maybe it was the best time to do that. I did not have children, a partner, or a mortgage—the responsibilities and commitments they'd both juggled while doing their PhDs.

At least, this is what I assumed they meant. Nothing tying me down, taking my energy or attention. Yet, all my life I'd felt the weight of considerable responsibility, to reconstruct a life that had been shattered into a million pieces, to understand why such a tragedy had happened to our family.

I could make the time to devote to a PhD; so many people said I should. I mused about the free time I'd lose if I devoted the next five to seven years to a degree: time with friends I would forego, writing I couldn't do, hobbies I wouldn't pursue, and adventures I couldn't take. The world seemed to close in as I imagined it. I thought about all I had accomplished, putting my education and career first. Doing what I was good at and what I was told, and staying strong and not falling down. I'd never really considered what I actually wanted to do with my life. But everything about the past two years had changed that.

During the first few years following my father's death, reporters would often ask how we children were doing. Family members, even our mother, said, "Oh, they're doing just fine." We were so clearly not fine. We *looked* fine, because we did what we were told and didn't cause any problems. We had internalized the expectation that we were doing well by everyone else's standards. God forbid we struggle with darkness, carrying the weight of murder on our little shoulders. God forbid we not be fine.

I smiled at my colleagues. Two years earlier, I would have gladly given my time and energy to the greater good of furthering understanding in my field through focused, observant research on some pressing issue related to youth work. Now, I thought of what my dad was trying to teach me, what he had been cultivating in his life before it was cut short.

I had a responsibility to do something with what I had learned these past two years. In that instant, it occurred to me that I deserved to have fun. So relaxed was my body that I could only say, "Thanks for your advice, guys. But I'm going to learn how to sail."

So one day I wandered the marina docks at Granville Island, where leisure boats were crammed next to one another, and found a sailing shop. I was perusing the nautical charts, cruiser guides, and class schedules when the woman behind the counter said, "How can I help you, hon?"

"Well," I said tentatively, "I used to sail a long time ago, in a past life. I was thinking that maybe I could learn the basics. See if I'm any good. I love the water, but I don't know a thing."

Her face lit up as I spoke. "Well, you're in the right place," she said. "I have the same story, dear. Started back up in my early thirties too. The best thing I could have done for myself. Haven't stopped since." She smiled. "You're in the right place."

So I signed up for sailing lessons, and came home each weekend with my thighs covered in well-earned bruises, which I proudly showed off to friends. After eight hours each day on the water, my body was exhausted. I learned to tie a bowline. I tried desperately to understand the physics of the wind. I watched the boats heel so far into the horizon that I distrusted my instructor's promise: "The boat will right itself. It is what it's designed to do."

A few weeks later, I passed theory tests, having memorized too many sailing terms, and was ready for my practical exam.

Our instructor smiled as he stood before us in the cabin. "Well, you've learned the science of sailing," he began. "You've proven yourselves capable. Now," he said with a mischievous smile that I was certain only sailors possess, "you're going to learn its art."

Each student took their turn demonstrating a safety maneuver and all points-of-sail. I was last in line. We shuffled our seats in the cockpit and I sat at the helm. I found myself instructing my fellow students: "Loosen the main sail for a beam reach" and then "Tighten the sheets for a close reach." My ease with this new language surprised me. They followed my directions. We moved a little faster with the wind.

Then everything seemed to quiet in my head. I was at the helm, my muscles engaged, perched on the hard seat of the cockpit, one hand on the tiller. The wind struck bodies, and we braced ourselves and held tight. I could feel my father watching me. Ocean spray hit my face, the waves crashed into the hull, and still the boat moved forward.

Crash, we cut into the waves.

Lift, the sails tightened.

Lean, she moved with the wind.

Until the day my father died, eleven years after my first summer on the ocean, everything had been an adventure. Adventure dies alongside those who it embodies, requesting, silently begging, to be resurrected. How do you truly remember someone? How do you feel what he felt, learn what he knew? How do you bring adventure back to life?

Now I felt what had drawn him in. I could no longer have him next to me, but I could do what he did, live what he lived, and make it my own. In doing so, perhaps I could know him differently, more fully than I ever could have if he'd been here next to me. Perhaps I could discover the adventure on my own.

"Ready to tack." I prepared my fellow students and moved to the opposite side, holding the tiller still at centre.

"Ready," they called out and held their sheets.

As I pulled the tiller close to my body, the boat swiftly turned to port. I watched the horizon. Waiting as she got into a good position for a close haul—with the Salish Sea to the west, the mountains to the north, Stanley Park to the east, and Vancouver to the south—I pushed the tiller back out to centre. She heeled. Wind caught the sails, and we moved forward. I breathed in the salty air.

I used the horizon to guide me, the wind to tell me where I could go, and the sails to get me there.

Finally, ever so alive, I found my way through.

EPILOGUE

In October 2014, eighteen months after I wrote my last letter to Sheldon, I observed my first Parole Board of Canada hearing. He applied for three types of unescorted temporary absences: community service, personal development, and extended twenty-four- to seventy-two-hour leaves from the prison grounds.

Four of us—my mom, her friend, one of my sisters, and me—arrived at the prison, where we checked in with the guards sitting in the administration building, and followed the communications officers as they escorted us to the newly built annex. We felt the crisp Alberta air on our cheeks as we walked along the path between buildings, passing the houses where minimum-security prisoners lived together in small groups. In front of a few of them, prisoners stood about casually, watching us pass by.

As we sat in the breakout room across from the boardroom where the hearing would take place, the communications officers oriented us to the proceedings.

"There will be a number of people in the room. Two parole board members will sit on one side of the table, and on the other side will be the offender, his parole officer who works in the prison, and a community representative of his choice. There will also be someone who introduces the proceedings and security guards at the door."

"Are my dad's brothers here?" I asked.

"Not to my knowledge," one of the officers said.

I took comfort in this news.

"I see that you did not submit Victim Impact Statements?" she asked while shuffling through her files.

"No, we didn't."

Victims may only speak at the hearing if they've written a Victim Impact Statement and submitted it to the Parole Board at least a month before the hearing. It has to be seen in advance by the offender. It is, after all, the offender's hearing. *Do not address the offender directly, but instead address the Board members who make the decision*, the fact sheet informs victims on submitting a statement to the board.

"As observers, you are not permitted to speak. You will sit in the chairs along the wall, and I'll escort you in and out of the room. At no point will the offender see you. He is not allowed to turn around. He will be brought into the room before you and taken out after you. He cannot address you directly, only through the parole board members."

I tried to imagine the room.

"Because it's not his first hearing, the parole board members typically don't spend too much time on the crime itself. Rather, they'll focus more on the offender's risk to re-offend, his progress with his rehabilitation."

Sheldon was already seated as we entered the boardroom. We sat in the designated chairs as instructed, five feet behind him.

Despite our expectation that the board members would not focus on the crime itself, they spent a considerable amount of time, at least forty-five minutes, asking him detailed questions.

"Why did you go toward the noise upstairs instead of leaving the house?"

"I don't know."

"Why did you pick up the kitchen knife?"

"I don't know."

"Why didn't you just leave?"

"I don't know," he said again. "I wanted to leave the house with something."

I quickly tired of "I don't know." In spite of twenty-two years of incarceration and eight letters from me detailing the effects of his crime and informing him of the essence of the man he killed, he seemed to have limited ability to integrate that information into what he was expected to demonstrate at this hearing.

"Who are your victims?"

"His wife ..." the offender started. "His brothers," he went on. "And his children."

I noted that he did not say my father was a victim of his crime, and he did not refer to the more than 1,000 people who attended his memorial services, the community he terrified, or my father's future patients, friends, and grandchildren.

"What is the long-term impact of your crime on the victims?"

"He's not there for Christmas," he said. "Or birthdays." That was it.

I thought of our exchanges, and it occurred to me that, of course, he couldn't say what the impact was. He'd never known what a father is or could be.

"Did you know your victim?"

"No," he responded.

"You were treated by him at the hospital?"

"I don't remember," he said.

I cringed and wondered again if he had been lying to me during our meeting. Or was he conveniently omitting information to the board in an effort not to show further culpability for the crime he took thirteen years to admit to? I wanted to speak up but knew I wasn't allowed.

"It says here," a board member noted, looking through his files on his laptop, "that you were in contact with one of your victims."

My eyes widened, knowing from the restorative justice practitioners that our correspondence was not to be mentioned during the hearings. I also remembered, from our letters and conversations, that he and I had agreed we could tell anyone we wanted about our exchanges.

"Yes," he said.

"How long were you in contact for?"

"About a year," he said.

I furrowed my brows, confused.

"What impact did your crime have on this victim?"

"Sadness. Nightmares," the offender said, despite the fact I never told him about any nightmares.

I wanted to interrupt, but I didn't know if I'd be removed from the room. I reluctantly stayed silent and stared directly at the board members, trying to will them to stop talking about me.

"What did that provide her?" a board member asked.

"Maybe some closure," he said.

I recalled what I had told him about my poor opinion of the concept of closure. My jaw clenched. I ruminated over the fact that he was allowed to interpret my experience and relay incorrect information without me being allowed to speak and to contradict it. I reminded myself that this was not a trial or a conversation, but rather, a one-sided hearing where the offender could claim anything he wanted, and it was up to the board to review the extensive information, weigh his comments, and make the decisions.

"What will you do on your weekend releases?"

"Maybe I'll go to Calgary," he said.

"Do you know anyone there?"

"Maybe I'll contact a friend of my family's."

"Have you contacted them already?"

"No."

"Then what will you do in Calgary?"

He did not respond.

Back in the breakout room, we reflected on the hearing while the board deliberated.

"Do you think he'll get it?" my mother asked.

"He needs a social worker in there," I said. "They'll approve the work and counselling, but they won't approve the extended unescorted leaves. It wasn't a good enough plan."

Sure enough, the board approved the work and counselling leaves, but not the extended weekend leaves. Not a good enough plan.

I shook my head, disappointed that he seemed unprepared to answer the most predictable of questions, that he did not demonstrate growth, and that he was inconsistent with what he had written to me, but most of all I was disappointed that I had to stay silent.

In April 2015, a year later, we attended another hearing. Comforted by already being familiar with the procedure, we moved easily from breakout room to boardroom to breakout room and back again. We listened to similar questions asked by different board members, more detailed than those asked by any police or prosecutor I'd heard. This time, the offender was applying for day parole.

"How will day parole be different for you?" a board member asked.

"It will be similar to my work releases, but I'll have the weekends free," the offender said.

While the board was encouraging and acknowledged his progress, they concluded that his plan was *underdeveloped and not viable*, citing limited positive social supports, including an estranged family, and the need *to gain further credibility* through escorted and unescorted temporary absences.

"Do you think he understands?" This is a question that is commonly asked of us when we return from these hearings.

"I think he understands the best that he can," I always say. "And that is not good enough."

In March 2016, Sheldon applied again for day parole, and the Parole Board of Canada held another hearing to consider his application. This time I brought Shannon, my curious and loving friend, to witness the process. The board focused on Sheldon's plan. He outlined a job he had secured through previous employment and a back-up job, in case of expected layoffs. He told the board of his new girlfriend and her son who lived in a nearby town.

Shannon and I nudged each other when we heard this news.

I was pleasantly surprised to see a new, professionally dressed parole officer sitting alongside Sheldon. They articulated a thorough plan, and the offender gave more forthcoming responses to the board's questions.

"Just how many break-and-enters were you doing at the time?"

"Hundreds over the years, maybe one a night," he confirmed, contrary to the few he'd acknowledged in previous hearings.

"What is the long-term effect of your crime on your victims?"

"He's not there for all of the cuddles and—" His voice started breaking. "All the moments." He paused. "It was me. It was all me."

I sighed in relief.

The parole board soon reported its decision:

> Throughout the hearing today, you presented as an open book, holding nothing back, and verbalizing an insight that goes considerably further than what is contained in the progressively positive information on file. Without pausing to take a breath, you immediately launched into listing your risk factors and strongly stated that you know exactly what they are. You actively

and fully participated in your hearing, asking appropriate questions and showing a genuine desire to understand the process and lay everything out in the open.

His application for day parole was approved for six months and as of this writing, continues to be approved at six-month increments through file review.

There is a legislated hearing for full parole set for August 2017, the month before the twenty-fifth anniversary of my father's death. I hope that this will be the offender's last hearing; I expect him to be released. Although he will be supervised for the rest of his life and, I am told by one communications officer, will be the "property of Correctional Services Canada until thirty days after his death," his full release into the community after a gradual reintegration over many years means he will be free.

At the same time, I will have given birth to my first baby. The following month, in September 2017, as the offender is released into the community, my family and my father's friends will gather at Larson Bay to celebrate my dad's great life, now scattered among the stories we carry forward. I will hold my newborn boy and tell him stories of his Grandpa Geoffrey. My son will know him, learn from him, and lovingly carry him forward as he grows and begins his own adventures in this painful, joyful, and beautifully complicated world.

She hopes that one day, soon after he leaves the prison on full parole, he will find himself in a park, breathing in the crisp Alberta air, feeling the heat of the bright prairie sun on his back. His girlfriend will be sitting on a park bench, leisurely reading and occasionally looking up to watch him push her son on the swing.

"Higher," the son may say.

He pushes her son higher and listens to him squeal in delight. The child feels the wind on his face as he swings forward, and the sensation of the sudden drop of the swing as it returns. He pushes him again.

She imagines that he will smile effortlessly, because he is free from the constraints that have held him back and because he sees his future before him. Where the world slows down for a moment, within the push and fall of the swing, he will see that life exists in the space between them.

Only then, it occurs to her, a world away from him, will he truly know what he took away.

Geoffrey Cragg in Whistler, British Columbia.
(Photo courtesy of Antoinette Choppin.)

ACKNOWLEDGMENTS

Many people make it possible for a book to come into being. You've all led me here, and this truly is a lovely space. Writing is performed in isolation but never alone. Thank you.

To Brian Lam and the team at Arsenal Pulp Press, I could not think of a better home for this story to be held. Thank you, Sonja and Trena, for leading me in their direction. Robyn So, thank you for your precise observations and astute direction to tighten the story's threads, carve and layer its shape, and help open up the story to shine brighter than I ever could have done alone. To Rebecca Coates for polishing an early draft so I could move it forward, and to Leighan Crowe for your generous beta-reader contribution. To Lemn Sissay, for allowing me to use your stunningly captivating poem, thank you.

Thank you to the editors of *48° North: The Sailing Magazine*, SFU's *emerge 14* anthology, the *Globe and Mail*, *The Places We've Been: Field Reports from Travelers Under 35*, and *Understorey Magazine* for publishing and holding space for earlier drafts of a handful of chapters, vignettes, and stories now held here.

To Mette Bach, I'm so happy I took your course. To the writing mentors in SFU's Creative Writing Department and Writer's Studio— Wayde Compton, Charles Demers, and Amber Dawn—thank you for your mentorship, feedback, encouragement, and most of all, faith. Wayde, thank you for asking for the rest of the story.

To my writing group members in The Writer's Studio Narrative Nonfiction group (Sonya, Katherine, Leanne, Margreet, Sheila, Kelly, Kelly, Charlotte, and Nikki), in The Writer's Studio Graduate Workshop (Joanne, Kelly, Lorraine, and Karen), and in the Banff Emerging Writers Creative Nonfiction group (Christa, Michelle, Baj, Anna, Miranda, Louise, Larissa, and Wayne), thank you for your ideas, feedback, and encouragement to move our stories forward. To Kelly Ryan, for our dares and evening blurb-writing sessions. How wonderful it is to have intersected with all of your work and your creative minds.

To Kristy Dellebuur O'Connor, Jennifer White, and Daniel Scott, for permitting me early on to write with a creative voice in the academic world. To Petra, Madelaine, and Shannon, for sparking possibilities. To Barry Lindahl for so long ago encouraging me to write challenging ideas well.

To Shannon McGeehan, for asking me the right question at the right time and in the right space; I would not have had this experience at this time in this way and in this space without your curiosity. To Dave, Jennifer, Sandi, and Susan, thank you for carrying my words across a mountain range and delivering them to the person who ruined my world. Your work is transformative because you trusted that I knew what I needed. To all Victims of Crime, may you, too, say what you need to and experience justice.

To my family, biological, blended, in-law, waiting to become, and yet to be, thank you for making space for my way of being. I look forward to many more joyful stories as our lives collectively move forward. Kip, our discussion of sailing terms brought a new level to the book's meaning. To my friends, thank you for seeing me and celebrating my choices. I can only hope I do the same for you.

And finally, to my father, who saw who I was long before I knew who that was; how lucky I am to bring your extraordinary soul forward.

Chapter 24 contains the spoken-word poem performed at the 2012 Vancouver International Writers Fest by Lemn Sissay, "Mourning Breaks," *Morning Breaks in the Elevator.* Edinburgh, UK: Canongate Books, 1999. Reprinted by permission of Don't Panic Projects.

Earlier drafts of some chapters were originally published in a different form by the author in the following publications:

"At the Helm." *48° North: The Sailing Magazine*, January 2015, 52–54. http://48north.com/48-north-january-2015/. Reprinted by permission of the publisher.

"Constructing a Life after Death." Master's thesis, University of Victoria, BC, 2008.

"My Father's Killer Has Been Granted Parole and I Am Relieved," Facts and Arguments, *Globe and Mail*, July 26, 2016. Reprinted by permission of the publisher.

"Preparing for a Lesser-Known Journey." In *The Places We've Been: Field Reports from Travelers under 35*, edited by Asha Veal Brisebois, 199–210. Chicago, IL: The Places We've Been Books, 2013. Reprinted by permission of the publisher.

"Then He Would Know." *emerge 14: The Writer's Studio Anthology*, 39–43. Burnaby, BC: Simon Fraser University Publications, 2014. Reprinted by permission of the publisher.

"Waiting to Be Heard." *Understorey Magazine*, no. 8 (2016). http://understoreymagazine.ca/article/waiting-to-be-heard/. Reprinted by permission of the publisher.

Geoffrey and Carys Cragg on the Salish Sea, Autumn 1983.
(Photo courtesy of the Cragg family.)

GLOSSARY OF CANADIAN CRIMINAL JUSTICE TERMS

Correctional Service Canada (CSC). The federal agency responsible for administering sentences over two years. The CSC manages correctional institutions and supervises offenders who are on parole.

Crown or state. In a court, the government lawyer prosecuting the accused in a criminal case. The Crown or state (government) represents the public interest, not the victim's, in these proceedings.

day parole. A means of preparing an inmate for full parole or statutory release. It allows an offender to participate in community-based activities and to spend evening and night hours at the institution or at a half-way house. Day parole is granted for up to six months at a time. Those serving life sentences may apply for day parole three years before their full parole eligibility date.

faint hope clause. The *Criminal Code* provision, introduced in 1976, allowing an inmate, after serving fifteen years of a life sentence, to apply for a review of the parole ineligibility period set when sentenced to life imprisonment. If the application was accepted, it was reviewed by a jury made up of residents from the community where the crime was committed. In 2011, this clause was repealed by *Bill S-6*.

full parole. A means of serving the remainder of a sentence in a community under supervision and specific conditions. Those serving life sentences for first degree murder may apply for full parole after serving twenty-five years. Those serving life sentences for second degree murder may apply after serving ten to twenty-five years, depending on the number set by the court at sentencing.

murder. "Culpable homicide" in the *Criminal Code*, R.S.C. ch. C-34, s. 212 (1985), "where the person who causes the death of a human being (i) means to cause his death, or (ii) means to cause him bodily harm that he knows is likely to cause his death, and is reckless whether death ensues or not." The sentence length and timing of eligibility for early conditional release are set by the sentencing judge to reflect the seriousness of the crime and the offender's level of responsibility for it. First and second degree murder convictions carry mandatory life sentences.

parole. Conditional release that is granted by the Parole Board. Four types of parole are available at different points in a sentence and involve graduated degrees of supervision. See *temporary absence, day parole,* and *full parole.* The fourth, statutory release, is not available to inmates serving life sentences.

Parole Board of Canada (PBC). An independent federal institution made up of members appointed from the community. It is concerned with the length of sentence that is served *in prison* and with the terms and timing of an inmate's release into the community to serve the remainder of the sentence. The board must weigh the benefit of early release to the offender versus the benefit/risk of early release to the community.

restorative justice. A model that focuses on identifying harms, empowering victims, and responding to both victims' and offenders' needs. In 1990, a pioneer of the model, Dr. Howard Zehr, proposed a new definition for crime: "Crime is a violation of people and relationships. It creates obligations to make things right. Justice involves the victim, the offender, and the community in a search for solutions that promote repair, reconciliation and reassurance."

retributive justice. The model on which Canada's criminal justice system is based. The definition of crime focuses on the offender and the community. Criminologist Dr. Howard Zehr defines crime as "a violation of the state, defined by lawbreaking and guilt. Justice determines blame and administers pain in a contest between the offender and the state directed by systematic rules."

temporary absence. Escorted or unescorted leave, usually for a finite length of time. Known by the acronyms ETA (escorted temporary absence) and UTA (unescorted temmporary absence), they allow an inmate to access medical treatment, participate in community service work, work-release programs, and counselling, and to have contact with family.

victim. In the *Canadian Victims Bill of Rights*, 2015 S.C. ch. 13, s. 2, one "who has suffered physical or emotional harm, property damage or economic loss as the result of the commission or alleged commission of an offence." For registered victim, see *victims' rights*.

Victim Impact Statement (VIS). A voluntary statement to the Court or subsequently to the Parole Board explaining the impact of a crime. Any person who is harmed by an offence may submit a VIS, giving details that may range from personal and emotional harm and physical injuries to property damage and financial losses. The Court will consider the VIS when determining sentencing.

victim-offender mediation. Focuses on the harms done rather than on the laws broken. Also known as victim-offender reconciliation, its programs are designed to respect both victim and offender and to involve and support them equally. In Canada, the Victim-Offender Mediation Program was started in British Columbia in 1991, and Restorative Opportunities was started in 2003 to make victim-offender mediation more available across the country.

victims' rights. Legislated recognition of victims' voices in the criminal justice system. Prior to a 1988 amendment to the *Criminal Code*, there were places in the criminal justice system for the accused, police, Crown and defense attorneys, judge, and parole officer, but there was no place for victims of an accused's alleged offence beyond being a witness for the Crown. In 2015, enactment of the *Canadian Victims Bill of Rights* broadened the definition of victim and clarified their rights, for example, that they and their familes deserve to be treated with courtesy, compassion, and respect. Victims may register with Correctional Service Canada and the Parole Board of Canada and ask to receive information about the offender. Examples of information include the offender's name, sentence length, institution location, parole eligibility dates, Parole Board hearing dates, Parole Board decisions, the nature of any conditions attached to the offender's release, the destination of the offender upon release, and whether the offender is in custody. Victims may attend Parole Board hearings as observers, access written copies of the board's decisions, and prepare and present a Victim Impact Statement to the board.

victim services. Programs to help victims navigate the criminal justice system, learn specific information about their rights, and find organizations that can address their needs for medical or financial services, for housing, and for emotional support. Programs and services for victims are developed and run by government organizations such as CSC and by for-profit and not-for-profit agencies such as CJI.

BIBLIOGRAPHY

Chapter Three

Beatty, Rob, and Rob Collins. "Hunt for Killer." *Calgary Herald,* September 18, 1992.

Collins, Rob. "Suspect Charged in Doctor's Killing." *Calgary Herald,* September 19, 1992.

Dolik, Helen. "Accused Killer Fingers Best Friend for Crime." *Calgary Herald*, July 9, 1993.

Dolik, Helen. "Accused Killer Sticks to Story." *Calgary Herald*, July 15, 1993.

_____. "Doctor's Murderer Sentenced to Life Term." *Calgary Herald*, July 17, 1993.

_____. "Murder Jury Still Out." *Calgary Herald*, July 16, 1993.

_____. "Shoeprint Left at Scene." *Calgary Herald*, July 7, 1993.

Jaremko, Gordon. "Murderer Appeals Sentence." *Calgary Herald*, September 17, 1994.

Kaufman, Bill. "MD's Widow Thanks City for Support." *Calgary Sun*, July, 18, 1993.

Martin, Kevin. "Murder Suspect's Claim Called Hoax." *Calgary Sun*, July 16, 1993.

_____. "Killer's Sentence Upheld." *Calgary Sun*, April 26, 1995.

Sollid, Leif. "Intruder Stabs Doctor to Death." *Calgary Sun*, September 17, 1992.

Chapter Twenty-Two

Coons, Cal, and Steve Lucas, writers. "Killer Gloves," *Exhibit A: Secrets of Forensic Science*. Season 3, episode 7. 1999. Directed by Ann Harbron and Deborah Samuel. Canada, 1999.

Chapter Twenty-Eight

Her Majesty the Queen v. Sheldon Thane Klatt (July 16, 1993), Calgary 9301-0329-CO (Alberta Queen's Bench). Courtesy of Justice Canada.

Epilogue

Parole Board of Canada, Prairies Region. Letter to author, March 23, 2016, p. 6. Courtesy of Justice Canada.

Glossary

Canada. "Acts, Regulation and Policy." Correctional Service Canada. Last modified May 15, 2013. http://www.csc-scc.gc.ca/about-us/index-eng.shtml.

Canada. *Canadian Victims Bill of Rights.* Justice Laws Website. Last modified April 20, 2017. http://laws-lois.justice.gc.ca/eng/acts/C-23.7/page-1.html.

Canada. *Criminal Code.* Justice Laws Website. Last modified April 20, 2017. http://www.laws-lois.justice.gc.ca/eng/acts/C-46/page-52.html#h-77.

Canada. "Parole Board of Canada." Parole Board of Canada. Last modified April 24, 2017. https://www.canada.ca/en/parole-board.html.

Canada. "Victims Guide to Information Services." Parole Board of Canada. Last modified October 13, 2016. https://www.canada.ca/en/parole-board/services/victims/victim-s-guide-to-information-services.html.

Fraser Region Community Justice Initiatives Association. "Restorative Justice: Justice Which Heals." Community Justice Initiatives Association. http://www.cjibc.org/home.

Zehr, Dr. Howard. *Changing Lenses: A New Focus on Crime and Justice*. Windsor, ON: Herald Press, 1990.

PHOTO: DAVID P. BALL

CARYS CRAGG is an instructor in Child, Family, and Community Studies at Douglas College in Coquitlam, British Columbia. Her personal essays, reviews, and short memoir have appeared in *The Globe and Mail, The Tyee,* and *Understorey,* among other publications. She is a graduate of The Writer's Studio at Simon Fraser University. *Dead Reckoning* is her first book. She lives in Vancouver.

caryscragg.com